The Third Eye

D1337528

To reflect the importance of supervision, and to widen understanding of its many facets, this book brings together not only the thoughts of some of the most experienced practitioners of group analysis, but also the reactions of those they have supervised. This assembly of knowledge will be of value to anyone who has to supervise others responsible for groups, whether within or beyond the boundaries of psychoanalysis.

The contributors examine areas such as the trainee's view of supervision, supervision within the NHS, block training courses at home and abroad, and the training and evaluation of supervisors. The book concludes with a supporting reference bibliography of relevant articles and books on supervision of group psychotherapy.

The Third Eye provides a detailed and practical exposition of one of the most important but least documented skills required of those practising in the expanding discipline of group analysis. The relevance of the material extends far beyond its field of origin. It will be of significant interest to a wide readership of those concerned with the training, assessment and development of others working with or having responsibility for groups.

Meg Sharpe is a Training Group Analyst and Supervisor at the Institute of Group Analysis, London. Also trained as an Analytical Psychologist, she runs a private practice and consultancy working with both groups and individuals at the Group-Analytic Practice, London.

The International Library of Group Psychotherapy and Group Process

General Editor: Dr Malcolm Pines
Institute of Group Analysis, London, and formerly of the Tavistock Clinic, London.

The International Library of Group Psychotherapy and Group Process reflects the group-analytic approach to psychotherapy from both practical and theoretical viewpoints. It takes into account developments in related areas and includes important works in translation.

The Third Eye

Supervision of Analytic Groups

Edited by Meg Sharpe

London and New York

First published 1995
by Routledge
11 New Fetter Lane, London EC4P 4EE

Simultaneously published in the USA and Canada
by Routledge
29 West 35th Street, New York, NY 1001

Typeset in Times by LaserScript, Mitcham, Surrey
Printed and bound in Great Britain by
Biddles Ltd, Guildford and King's Lynn

British Library Cataloguing in Publication Data
A catalogue record for this book is available from the British Library

Library of Congress Cataloging in Publication Data
A catalogue record for this book has been requested

ISBN 0–415–10634–6 (hbk)
ISBN 0–415–10635–4 (pbk)

Contents

Figures

Contributors

Malcolm Pines began his psychoanalytic training while still a medical student. He went to the Maudsley Hospital to receive his analytic training from S. H. Foukes, and went from there to the Cassel Hospital to work under Tom Main. He later became Senior Lecturer in Psychotherapy at St George's Hospital, and following this, held consultant posts at the Maudsley Hospital and Tavistock Clinic. He has published articles and papers on most aspects of psychoanalysis and is prominent in international circles. He is editor of the International Library of Group Psychotherapy and Group Process. He is a founder member of the Institute of Group Analysis and the Group-Analytic Practice.

Harold L. Behr is Consultant Child and Family Psychiatrist at Central Middlesex Hospital, Middlesex, and practises at the North London Centre for Group Therapy. He teaches and supervises at the Institute of Group Analysis (IGA), and is a Training Group Analyst. He is the author of several articles in his field which have been translated and published in Danish, French and German.

Martyn Corbett read English at Cambridge and studied cinema with the British Film Institute under the auspices of London University. He taught English and media studies in further and higher education and completed IGA's Qualifying Course in 1992. He conducts therapeutic and staff support groups in the NHS and practises privately.

Lisbeth E. Hearst is a Training Group Analyst and Supervisor of the IGA, teaches on the IGA Qualifying Course, and is a past Chair of the IGA Overseas Training Committee. She conducts several overseas training courses in Group Analysis.

Rachel Brown trained at Bethlem and Maudsley Hospital. She is a Consultant Child and Family Psychotherapist in South West Herts, and lectures at the Tavistock Clinic and University College Hospital School of Medicine.

Meg Sharpe is an Analyst (Jungian – Society of Analytical Psychology) and an IGA Training Group Analyst and Supervisor. She is a Clinical Member of the American Group Psychotherapy Association and a past Chair of the IGA Training Committee. She has worked extensively in the NHS and overseas on training courses for the IGA, and is a Member of the Group-Analytic Practice.

Adele Mittwoch has a background in the natural sciences, and experience in industry and with the Medical Research Council. She trained with the British Association of Psychotherapists and with IGA. She is Treasurer of IGA and a member of the editorial board of the journal *Group Analysis.*

Vivienne Cohen, lately Senior Lecturer and Honorary Consultant Psychotherapist, St Bartholomew's Hospital and Medical College and Director of the Psychotherapy Unit. She trained at the Maudsley Hospital where she was Registrar to Dr S. H. Foulkes who was also her group analyst. She is a founder member of the Institute of Group Analysis, a past Chair of the Training Committee and an Honorary Member of the Group-Analytic Society.

Robin Sproul-Bolton came to psychotherapy and Group Analysis following a career as an army officer. After managing a Therapeutic Community for disturbed young adults, he joined the acute psychiatric unit of a district general hospital, the source of his contribution.

Morris Nitsun is District Psychologist and Specialist in Adult Psychotherapy in Redbridge Health Authority. He is a teaching member of IGA and Chair of the Institute's Scientific Programmes Committee, and author of numerous articles on Group Analysis and psychotherapy.

Jane Knowles is Consultant Psychotherapist to the Winterbourne Therapeutic Community, presently situated in Fair Mile Hospital, South Oxfordshire, and a 'Medical Director who gardens'. She is a practising Group Analyst, and an Associate of the Group-Analytic Practice.

Per A. Føyn was a General Practitioner when he started IGA Block Training in Oslo. He is now a member of the teaching staff of the Norwegian IGA and head of a secure unit for violent and psychotic patients at Gaustad Hospital, Oslo.

Felix Schwarzenbach is a psychiatrist at the University of Bern Social Psychiatric Unit, Switzerland. He trained in Group Analysis at the Seminar for Group Analysis in Zurich and his special interest is in groups with psychotic patients. He was a Research Fellow for the Swiss National Foundation for Science, at the Medical Research Council.

Stephen Cogill has worked in the health services for twenty years and is District Chief Psychologist. He is also in private practice as a group analyst, and has been teacher and Supervisor at the IGA for the past ten years. He has researched the mother–infant relationship and the significance for the child of a depressed mother.

Yannis K. Tsegos is a graduate and member of the IGA London, is President of the IGA (Athens) and Director of training and research at the Open Psychotherapeutic Centre, which he founded. He works in private practice and is active on several international bodies, including the European Group-Analytic Training Institutions Network.

Victoria Graham Fuller is a member of the Institute of Group Analysis in London. She is also a Professional Member of the Society of Analytical Psychology and is in private practice as a Jungian Analyst. She teaches and supervises for a number of London training bodies.

Marlene Spero graduated in and taught Sociology before moving into the world of Management Development and Training. She trained as a group analyst and now works in private practice and as a consultant to organisations. She is a member of the IGA's General Introductory Course in London and Israel, and Chair of the Applied Section of the IGA.

Maggie Wood is a freelance librarian who has worked for the Institute of Group Analysis since 1983.

Editor's acknowledgements

I would like to thank all the contributors to this book for so generously sharing their experiences of the many different aspects of group-analytic supervision.

Special thanks are also due to our students and group members, past and present, who have stimulated and broadened our learning.

Introduction

Malcolm Pines

I give a warm welcome to this book in the series of the International Library of Group Psychotherapy and Group Process, for it breaks new ground. Theory and therapy in training are transferred into practice when the student begins to work alone with the patient group. The loneliness and anxiety that this brings out in many, if not all, students is well conveyed in some of the vividly written accounts by students themselves.

At the Institute of Group Analysis the method is to train therapists to work alone; co-therapy is not the training model as it is in many other training situations and we are often asked why we keep to this model when there are many advantages to co-therapy, such as sharing the field of observation, offering patients the opportunity to work out family transferences with two parental figures, a continuity of treatment if one therapist is ill or away, therapists sharing the burden, particularly with the more disturbed patients. The reasons for our model can clearly be seen in the sensitive and deep accounts by the student therapists of their experiences and how they have learnt to understand and use them.

What is unique and particularly valuable in the Institute of Group Analysis training is well illustrated in accounts by both supervisors and supervisees. In Chapter 6 Vivienne Cohen clearly and sensitively monitors her students' work and in her reports we can follow the progress – or lack of it – of her supervisees. She demonstrates the effective use of confrontation with supervisees who are denying or rationalising their problems. She also describes the use of information that comes from the supervision situation which then goes to the Training Committee and may, in some instances, be given to the training group analyst who may, or may not, choose to make use of it. No doubt there will be some training institutions where such information flow is not allowed, so that the confidentiality and self-enclosure of the therapy group is protected. In the Institute of Group Analysis we have tended to allow and to value this permeability of boundaries as the training takes place within a training community, a large group where information flow and exchange is valuable, indeed essential.

Readers of the supervision accounts will gain an impression of the firm holding and containment that supervision provides and which generations of students have needed and appreciated.

At the end of training, students are required to write a clinical paper describing their training group experiences, and outlining their understanding of the group process. These are often sensitive and deep accounts of the therapists' personal experiences, of difficulties, and their growing capacities to deal with the many stressful situations they often find themselves in. Frequently they are able to link these experiences as therapists in their own therapy groups with their experiences in their personal group-analytic therapy and events in their training groups. In effect they become self-supervisors, internalising the therapeutic and training experiences. Some of these learning experiences are clearly seen in the contributions of Martyn Corbett, Per Føyn, Rachel Brown and Felix Schwarzenbach.

There are few accounts of supervision in group analysis, far fewer than in psychoanalysis. Partly this is because group-analytic training has a much shorter history and there are only a few training institutes. Our own knowledge about our capacity for supervision is comparatively young and Meg Sharpe provides a useful outline of how to go about the task of setting up a supervision situation. It is indeed refreshing to see the variety of methods that she uses, and the reader can readily appreciate the stimulation supervisees can get from her flexible approach. The full-length presentation of one of her supervision sessions is a fascinating and rich example of group-analytic experience, showing the creative use of the group-analytic stance in a difficult situation and how the student was helped by the responses of the members of her supervision group.

In supervision of dyadic therapy much has been made of the concept of 'parallel process', the emergence in supervision of phenomena that parallel those in the treatment situation. Although these do undoubtedly occur, I often feel that these parallel situations as described have a certain artificiality to them, that we expect them to occur and that when they are not happening we make them happen. The group-analytic examples described seem to me very convincing as the group situation itself acts as an amplifier, increasing the range and intensity of the supervisee's response.

Several contributors have brought out the intensity of the training experience, that of moving in a short period of time between being a patient, a supervisee, a pupil and a therapist. This process is amplified in the block training that the Institute of Group Analysis has instituted in Scandinavia, Switzerland and other countries, processes that Lisbeth Hearst and Harold Behr skilfully bring out. In block training the intense weekend experience is followed by weeks of lone activity, and how the trainees cope with this experience is reflected in their therapeutic styles which can range from exaggerated self-sufficiency and distancing from patients to hurt and angry feelings of abandonment which may affect the therapists and their work. However, when these feelings are recognised and surface, a considerable move in the learning process occurs.

This learning process, the essence of training, is aptly described by Per Føyn as dealing with 'dumb spots' and 'blind spots': dumb spots are areas of ignorance that can be remedied by working hard at learning relevant information, blind spots need a different form of work, the personal insight that comes through therapy and supervision. This distinction is again well brought out by Yannis Tsegos, who convincingly describes the way in which knowledge grows: the process of unlearning existing knowledge, becoming free to absorb rich and complex new experiences, many of which come about in supervision. In supervision the students are relating to the objects of knowledge – the groups presented – but the learning largely concerns the subjects, the trainees, their experiences in the supervisory situation. The Athens model of supervision is a real group-analytic innovation that bears study and adoption in other centres.

There are many memorable passages in these papers but I shall quote only one that supplies a suitable ending. It is from Harold Behr in Chapter 1:

> The group-analytic concept of the group as a figure–ground constellation, offering ever-changing configurations of dialogue, provides a useful working model and serves as an anchor for trainees who feel themselves tossed from one interaction to another in a group. In the end, the trainee usually comes to realise that 'good-enough' therapy depends not so much on knowing what is going on, but on being able to hold the setting, providing oneself as a containing presence, facilitating open communication between all in the group (including the conductor) and protecting the group from buffetings which threaten its predictability and safety.

I am confident that readers of this book will be able to obtain a closer look at group-analytic therapy and training than has previously been possible.

Chapter 1

The integration of theory and practice

Harold L. Behr

Supervision lies in the terrain between the teaching of theory and practice of therapy. As such, it allows for an integrated experience which combines the conceptual thinking of the former with the experiential learning of the latter. In supervision the supervisee's work comes under the benign scrutiny of the supervisor, enabling the two to focus together on the supervisee's skills and technique, and providing a major influence on the supervisee's overall professional development.

In the context of individual psychotherapy, supervision can be seen as a conversation between two persons about a third. However, the conversation is carefully structured, and the situation is complicated by the fact that the third person is never physically present. A series of relationships arises within a common matrix. The therapeutic relationship between supervisee and patient is brought into the supervision room through the reporting of material from the therapy sessions, and this in turn impinges on the supervisory relationship. Supervisor and patient are destined never to meet, yet each affects the other through the intermediacy of the therapist. The purpose of supervision is twofold: firstly, to catalyse the therapeutic relationship for the ultimate benefit of the patient, and secondly to enhance the supervisee's skills as a therapist. It is assumed that the supervisor has certain attributes, be they greater knowledge, experience or 'know-how', which can be imparted to the less knowledgeable, less experienced supervisee. Supervision therefore becomes a way of transmitting an accumulated body of knowledge and expertise from one generation of therapists to the next. It is a vehicle for the 'oral tradition' of the school of psychotherapy which it represents.

In the context of supervision for group psychotherapy, an analogous process occurs. Here the focus moves between the supervisee's therapeutic relationship with a group of patients (referred to in a training context as the training group) and the supervisory relationship, which may be with just one person (the supervisor) or with a whole group. The supervision group can be understood as a figure–ground constellation, the foreground of which is usually occupied by the interaction between the supervisee and the training group, while the background constitutes a kaleidoscopic pattern of configurations which connect the therapeutic relationship, the supervisory relationship and the wider training setting, including the supervisee's relationship with the training institute and the supervisee's own personal therapy group. From time to time any of these may emerge into the foreground and become a focus of dynamic work.

GROUP SUPERVISION IN THE CONTEXT OF GROUP-ANALYTIC TRAINING

It is easy to underestimate the degree of bewilderment and apprehension which engulfs trainees at the beginning of their group-analytic training. Moving uncertainly between the rarified atmosphere of unfamiliar theoretical ideas and the deep waters of personal therapy, the trainee often feels most grounded in the supervision group. Here, together with three or four fellow trainees and the supervisor, in an attitude of shared learning, group process can be looked at objectively, and techniques for intervening therapeutically can be rehearsed and understood within a dynamic matrix.

The model of training provided by the London Institute of Group Analysis offers a tripartite structure in which personal therapy, theory teaching and supervision are held within a single dynamic framework. Trainees are encouraged to regard the three components of the training as informing one another, and material from the one may become the subject of one or both of the other two. In practice, supervision is often the forum for this integrative process, since it is here that the trainees can make connections between their own work as therapists and the newly digested ideas emanating from the theory seminars. At the same time, the supervision group, composed as it is of individuals committed to an analytic understanding of groups, often captures the feelings generated by members of the supervisee's training group, reflecting them back to the supervisee and replicating a group dynamic which resonates with the patient group.

Feelings ran high in a group conducted by a male trainee after two women members of the group got into an irritable conflict over the marital difficulties of a man in the group. One identified fiercely with the man's partner, the other with the man himself. The conductor allowed the conflict to escalate, and a point was reached where one woman burst into tears and the other lapsed into a grim silence. The following week one of the women (the silent one) was absent, having sent a message that she was not well.

In the supervision, the trainee admitted to having felt paralysed by the conflict which had raised echoes of arguments between his parents when he was a child. He had justified his silence however, with the consoling thought that 'the feelings were all there in the group and the group seemed to be working well with the problem'. This generated a heated exchange amongst his peers, some of whom felt that he should have supported the more vulnerable-seeming woman (who had cried), others that the silent woman was more at risk of dropping out. The supervisor helped the group to look at the chain of events which had developed from the male group member's tendency to 'split' the group, through to the conductor's silent collusion with the process, to a similar scenario that was being replicated in the supervision group itself. This freed the trainee to acknowledge that he had private sympathy with the woman who had cried and that he could think now about the personal significance of this for him. The way was open for an exploration of these issues in his own therapy and the supervision group could address the task of retrieving the potential drop-out.

RECONCILING THEORY AND PRACTICE

Group analysis as a subject does not lend itself readily to teaching. The problem lies in the elusive character of those concepts which can be regarded as specific to group analysis (e.g. the group matrix, mirroring, resonance, and dynamic administration) and the many non-specific concepts which inform group-analytic thinking derived from well-established schools of discourse, such as psychoanalysis and systems theory. A large number of theoretical antecedents are therefore woven together in a single fabric, making it difficult for the neophyte group analyst to discern a coherent theoretical entity.

In practice, however, the hybrid organism which is group analysis has a clear and distinctive identity which distinguishes it from other models of group psychotherapy. The principle of investing the group as a whole with therapeutic potential, while never losing sight of the individual, lies at the core of group-analytic practice. Around this principle have developed an array of techniques, each of which is by no means specific to group analysis, but which cumulatively, and within the context of group therapy, amount to a distinctive therapeutic approach.

Learning, therefore, advances along a broad front, as the trainee acquires various techniques for addressing the multiplicity of practical and dynamic issues which can arise in groups and matches them with the many facets of group-analytic theory which underlie those techniques. In supervision, it is mainly the technical aspects of group analysis which are examined: preparing the ground for the group, interviewing, assessing and preparing potential group members, protecting the group setting from incursions, managing the group boundary, coping with difficult situations as they arise, steering the group towards a more reflective mode of functioning, and helping the group to make sense of the rich, confusing and emotionally charged material which contributes to the group process.

STRUCTURE AND DYNAMICS OF THE SUPERVISION GROUP

At the level of a Qualifying Course, our experience at the Institute of Group Analysis is that a mix of beginners and more advanced trainees works well. To some extent this composition of a supervision group reproduces the slow-open model of the therapy groups. Trainees have to welcome new members and say goodbye to old ones with the same ripples of feeling which run through a patient group over such issues as: 'What will the new person bring to the group?' 'Am I ready to leave?' 'Have I done well enough?' 'How will I continue to get support after I have left?' The vigilant supervisor will ensure that time is set aside to address these issues, and that the group of peers is mobilised to make its own dynamic contribution to the process.

Beginners' lack of clinical or therapeutic experience turns out to be a 'non-problem', as does the fact that the trainees come from diverse professional backgrounds. The group is made up of individuals who have been through a careful selection process and who almost invariably provide an immediate and constructive input into the supervision. All trainees will have been in their own personal therapeutic groups for at least a year prior to joining the formal training programme, and come to supervision equipped with a good sense of how to function in a group-analytic setting.

Occasionally trainees have to unlearn habits acquired in their core professions, and here the diversity of professional backgrounds provides a salutary opportunity for exchange transfusions between trainees. For example, those from a teaching background occasionally have to modify a tendency towards excessive structuring and didacticism; psychiatrists may have a proclivity for medicalising therapeutic problems, being too preoccupied with diagnostic categories, or taking inappropriate responsibility for the medical care of their patients (e.g. offering 'helpful' professional advice about medication, or illness). The multiprofessional composition of the supervision group rapidly neutralises these professional defences and frees the trainee to think and function in a more psychodynamic way.

The frequency, time scale and duration of the supervision sessions parallels that of the training group. The supervision group meets at weekly intervals for one and a half hours, and experiences the same rhythm of working periods and breaks as the training group. Because of the need to allow for detailed reporting of group process and discussion of group material by the trainees, it is necessary to structure the supervision sessions quite carefully. Enough time has to be set aside for peer group interaction while ensuring that all members of the supervision group have the opportunity to bring up issues concerning their training group and explore them in depth. Within these time constraints there has to be enough flexibility to accommodate discussions about the inevitable crises or acute problems which erupt from time to time in training groups. I find that the system which works best is one in which everyone has an opportunity to report on their group each session, some only briefly, perhaps for no more than a few minutes, others (not more than two) in substance and in depth, while anyone can claim additional time to deal with more pressing issues. Through a gradually rotating system of turn-taking for 'major' and 'minor' presentations, each trainee has a regular 'slot' for detailed attention to his or her group, and all are kept in touch with one another's groups. This does mean, however, that the supervisor has to be especially watchful of the time boundaries, and mindful of when to 'cue in' the peer group, when to invite a pause in the presentation (or 'freeze the action'), and when to offer comments.

Listening to the material from a session, I try to place myself in the trainee's shoes, monitoring my own possible interventions alongside those of the trainee's. What might I have said at that point? Would I have intervened just then? If our paths seem to be diverging, I might recapitulate the process as I have understood it and invite a response from the peer group. This opens up fresh dynamic insights and often achieves the reconciliation of contrasting perspectives.

It is especially important to acknowledge therapeutic competence. If a training group is functioning well, or if a trainee seems to be handling a particular situation effectively, I look for an opportunity to draw attention to this. Trainees feel affirmed by a supervision in which their strengths and skills, as well as their blind spots, are recognised. The awe of the training situation and the confusion intrinsic to group interaction can sometimes lead to unjustified feelings of pessimism and self-doubt, which positive feedback by the supervisor helps to counteract.

The actual reporting of material is as varied as the personalities of the trainees. Beginning trainees are given a structure in which they are encouraged to record as much of the raw material of the sessions as they can hold on to, capturing it in sequence as far as possible, and not bothering to analyse or 'package' it in theoretical terms. That task will be left to the supervision group. Trainees sometimes have to be prompted to remember and record their own interventions. Not infrequently a beautiful process account of a session is presented, from which the conductor's participation is conspicuously absent!

Trainees are encouraged to plot the group's attendance record week by week, from which it becomes possible to see at a glance the pattern of attendances, absences and latecomings. This provides a useful chart of the group's course through the turbulent waters of arrivals, departures, holiday breaks and other group events. Schematic representations of group sessions showing how people seat themselves can provide a useful prop for the presentation and can help the supervision group to visualise interpersonal interactions. In general, however, I discourage handouts which list biographical details of the individual group members, or record complicated psychodynamic or diagnostic formulations. Too often a preoccupation with this kind of information gets the supervision bogged down in a welter of facts which contribute little to an understanding of the group-analytic process.

As trainees become more experienced, the supervision group comes to feel more like a group of colleagues, sharing thoughts with one another about the complexities of group analysis. The group being presented becomes a focus for comparing notes on counter-transference and technique, and the realisation dawns that there is no definitively 'correct' intervention at any given point. The collective voice of the supervision group speaks clearly, as it does in a patient group.

I occasionally proffer my own experiences as a conductor (for better or worse) to the supervision group, setting them alongside those of the trainees. In a well-functioning supervision group the trainees come to realise that the training is designed, not to create clones of some imaginary, idealised group analyst, but to encompass a diversity of styles, techniques, and approaches.

THE DEMOLITION OF MYTHS ABOUT GROUP-ANALYTIC TECHNIQUE

Whether or not they have had previous experience of psychotherapy prior to entering their group-analytic training, most trainees bring with them assumptions about the sort of behaviour which constitutes good therapeutic practice. In their early endeavours as group conductors, they attempt to implement techniques which, by their reckoning, will move the group in the direction of the ideal. The supervision group has to provide a corrective learning experience without undermining the trainees' confidence in their skills. Often this amounts to no more than a nudge towards greater flexibility, allowing the pendulum to swing towards the midpoint between two polarities. Anxious beginners are notoriously rigid in their application of real and imagined rules. In a field as nebulous as group psychotherapy, it is always tempting to adhere to clear and dogmatic assumptions and to deal with uncertainty by adopting a handful of monolithic formulas in the hope of bringing some order to the confusion.

THE RETICENT THERAPIST

One of the commonest pitfalls facing the beginning group analyst lies in the tendency to withhold interventions to a point where the group starts to move in a counter-therapeutic direction. Sometimes this well-intentioned position is governed by an overzealous adherence to the group-analytic tenet that 'the group does the work', forgetting that the conductor is very much part of the group, and failing to realise that the group members, for all their inherent therapeutic capabilities, depend heavily on the conductor to actively mould the therapeutic culture towards an attitude of openness and interpersonal exploration, especially in the group's formative stages.

Another reason for therapeutic reticence lies in a misguided translation from psychoanalytic technique into group analysis, of the notion that the therapist should furnish a 'blank screen' to draw out transference projections. This therapeutic stance is sometimes fuelled by the therapist's genuine anxiety, a fear of saying or doing something that might interrupt a delicate process, and perplexity about what is really going on in the group. When in doubt, it is often easier to take refuge in silence, especially if one's silence can be justified by some respectable professional axioms.

PREOCCUPATION WITH THE GROUP AS A WHOLE AT THE EXPENSE OF THE INDIVIDUAL

Related to the problem of excessive reticence is an attitude which assumes that the therapist should confine interventions to pronouncements about the group as a whole. Often these pronouncements take the form of interpretations, another technique borrowed from classical psychoanalysis and from some forms of psychoanalytic group psychotherapy, and often used inappropriately or prematurely in an effort to hold the group to a psychoanalytic mode of functioning.

The problem with predominantly group-as-a-whole interventions, as with excessive reticence, is that individual group members are often left feeling unheld or unrecognised. Anxiety and frustration are increased, and group members find it more difficult to interact freely with one another in a mutually therapeutic mode or tolerate one person holding the focus for very long. Such groups tend to be affected by an increased drop-out rate and function with an anxious, compliant culture. Supervision in such a situation concentrates on encouraging the trainee to recognise the importance of acknowledging individuals, modelling dyadic interactions within the group, and increasing the repertoire of interventions to include not only interpretations but other forms of communication, and especially to feel free to ask occasional questions and offer affiliative comments. The challenge to therapeutic omniscience is, not surprisingly, often greeted with relief.

PREOCCUPATION WITH INDIVIDUALS AT THE EXPENSE OF THE GROUP

A contrasting, but equally hazardous course which some trainees embark upon is the overactive engagement with group members to the point where the rest of the group is forced into the background and loses effectiveness as a therapeutic agency. When a particular group member is chosen as the focus, the trail in supervision quickly leads to the conductor's counter-transference. It often becomes clear that the trainee's overidentification with a group member, or with a sub-group (the men, or the women, for instance), is shadowed by overidentification with a larger, archetypal symbolic representative of that person or sub-group, for example, 'the helpless little boy' or 'the vulnerable mother'. Equally, confrontation over the tendency to ignore some individuals and sub-groups may reveal a negative counter-transference. These counter-transference issues can then be usefully explored, along with other counter-transference issues, in the trainee's own therapy group, having been opened up in the supervision group.

It is difficult to know when to focus on the individual and when to focus on the group. The group-analytic concept of the group as a figure–ground constellation, offering ever-changing configurations of dialogue, provides a useful working model and serves as an anchor for trainees who feel themselves tossed from one interaction to another in the group. In the end, the trainee usually comes to realise that 'good-enough' therapy depends not so much on knowing what is going on, but on being able to hold the setting, providing oneself as a containing presence, facilitating open communication between all in the group (including the conductor) and protecting the group from buffetings which threaten its predictability and safety.

STEERING BETWEEN THE SCYLLA OF THE 'HERE AND NOW' AND THE CHARYBDIS OF THE 'THERE AND THEN'

Group analysts vary somewhat in the extent to which they facilitate the exploration of interactions between the group members themselves, as opposed to the exploration of material deriving from group members' relationships outside the group and past experiences. Excessive pre-occupation with either mode can constitute a group defence against open communication. Some trainee group analysts have a tendency to polarise along this spectrum as a means of resolving difficult therapeutic dilemmas. As group analysts, we have considerable power to influence the direction which a group takes, and it is not sufficient to plead that one should be guided by the group in this matter. Supervision helps the trainee to steer a middle course through these uncharted waters.

Quite often the supervision session is occupied with helping trainees to turn the rudder away from the 'here and now' (an interactional field which has much fascination for professionals but is usually of little interest to 'bona fide' patients), and steer the group towards material which brings alive the group members' own worlds outside the group. The introduction of this material into the group makes it available for therapeutic work and almost invariably engages the group. From time to time the rudder has to swing the other way, particularly when a group changes its membership, or when a group event, such as conflict between group members, intrudes into the process. But for the most part, groups function well in an atmosphere in which all can feel able to bring their outside lives and inner worlds into the space of the group to be held, looked at and worked on by the whole group.

THE VIRTUES OF SMALL TALK AND HUMOUR

Trainees often feel an obligation to maintain their groups at a 'profound' or 'analytic' level of communication. In practice this often leads to the creation of an unduly oppressive, solemn atmosphere in which group members feel uncomfortable about bringing to the group any material other than their most serious life problems or their most premeditated thoughts. Light-hearted or humorous comments may be frowned on as frivolous, or construed, implicitly or explicitly, as 'defensive'.

In supervision, I go to some lengths to foster a welcoming attitude towards humorous, joking, playful, or bantering interactions, redefining them as the adult equivalent of childhood play. I encourage trainees to look at them as creative opportunities for entering the transitional space of the group and I show them how to amplify such communications within the group, and how to induct group members into an exploration of their therapeutic significance. By the same token, trainees often have to be helped to elevate mundane forms of communication such as casual observations, exchanges of trivial information, gossip, generalisations, conversations about social and political issues in the world at large, seemingly petty remarks and throw-away lines, to the level of important contributions, with inherent therapeutic potential. It is not too difficult to demonstrate how any such interaction in the group, if grasped, can lead through a maze of associations, to deeper, emotionally charged levels of communication. Supervision also helps trainees to discard the assumption that it is analytically correct to withhold their own playful impulses and humorous inclinations.

INTERPRETATION OR INTERRUPTION?

Trainees generally experience relief as they come to appreciate the fundamental group-analytic tenet that the licence to interpret is granted not only to the conductor, but to individual group members, and to the group as a whole. The formal, elaborately constructed interpretation of classical psychoanalysis is replaced by a gradually emergent group response to group members' material. The concept of 'ego training in action' takes pride of place in the therapeutic repertoire, superseding interpretation by the conductor as the main therapeutic instrument. Moreover, as mentioned earlier, if interpretation is offered as the only therapeutic intervention by an otherwise inscrutable conductor, a passive, regressed group dynamic is cultivated, weakening the therapeutic potential of the group as a whole.

When the conductor does venture an interpretation, timing is of the essence. Trainees and seasoned therapists alike struggle with this problem. Too early an intervention, delivered with a ring of finality, and conveying all the power and authority of the therapist, can stifle an emerging dynamic. Similarly, an interpretation given as a means of effecting closure over a messy, unresolved interaction, can be experienced as a gratuitous offering, and may be aimed more at reducing the conductor's anxiety than at moving the group forward. The so-called 'plunging interpretation', an attempt to link group associations with primitive levels of communication before the group itself is ready to make the connection spontaneously, is another common, tempting but generally unhelpful intervention, and can be experienced by the group more as a puzzling interference than a facilitating contribution.

Trainees are also sometimes inclined to pull communication insistently towards themselves, in the belief that the conductor should be the central transference object. Conductor-centred interpretations may well be indicated, especially early in therapy, when an individual or the group has to be coaxed from an attitude of dependence towards a more mutually interdependent mode of communicating, but trainees often struggle to get the balance right between centrality and marginalisation, and inappropriately resort to making transference interpretations as a means of asserting their position in the group.

A group being held in a large psychiatric hospital was briefly interrupted when the door opened and an unkempt, bewildered-looking man wandered into the room. The conductor ushered him out, and one woman remarked indignantly that it was disgraceful that people could get lost like that in a hospital with no one nearby to keep an eye on them. A man in the group facetiously remarked that the man could have been a psychiatrist. This was greeted with peals of laughter which broke the tension, and a series of rapid-fire associations about how 'crazy' psychiatrists are and how, according to one group member, they are even more 'weird' than their patients. There was more laughter and joking, with references to the cannibal psychiatrist in the film *Silence of the Lambs*. Someone remarked drily that she did not consider herself a tasty morsel for any psychiatrist. The conductor delivered an interpretation to the effect that the group was coping with the anxiety of chaos and fear of madness by projecting this onto himself, the therapist. This was greeted with a long silence which was broken by an apparent *non sequitur* when someone remarked that time seemed to be going by very slowly and this seemed like one of the longest sessions he could remember. The session ended with two members announcing that they could not be there the following week because of family commitments. One group member mentioned that she would have to collect her young son from a friend since he could not find his way home by himself.

In the supervision, the trainee's peers reflected back to him that they felt angry on behalf of his group. The supervision session helped the trainee to focus on a number of issues: the group's anger at the intrusion into their setting and the conductor's failure to protect them from this, their identification with the man who was manifestly an inpatient at the hospital and therefore in need of more intensive therapy than they themselves required, with all the fears and wishes associated with this, including the fear of madness, which was indeed reflected in their attempts to project this on to the powerful figure of the psychiatrist/therapist. The supervision group debated the pros and cons of breaking into the jocular mode of the group with a solemn interpretation which had effectively widened the distance between the rest of the group and the conductor at a moment when the group was perhaps attempting to reconcile stereotyped differences between 'sanity' and 'madness'.

COPING WITH CRITICAL MOMENTS IN THE GROUP

The supervision group sometimes functions as a shock absorber when a training group experiences a crisis, or when a group event occurs which shocks or traumatises the group, such as the suicide or attempted suicide of a group member, the sudden appearance of severe mental disturbance or serious illness in a group member, or an episode of destructive acting-out behaviour.

A woman trainee telephoned her supervisor to ask for some urgent advice. She herself had been telephoned by a distressed group member who informed her that she had been found to have a breast lump which had proven to be malignant, and that she might have to undergo surgery. The group member doubted whether she could share this with the group, her manifest reason being that another group member's mother was critically ill with cancer, and that she did not want to add to that person's burden. She even wondered whether she would return to the group at all. The trainee herself had misgivings about this, fearing the impact on a group whose membership she was already experiencing as precarious, of a group member with a serious, potentially life-threatening illness. The supervisor supported the trainee in her decision to offer the group member an individual session as a prelude to returning to the group, and the supervision group encouraged the trainee to retain the group member and help both her and the rest of the group to deal with the shock of the news, the mourning of the loss of good health, the anxiety about the future, and possible repercussions on other group members. In fact, the group worked well with these issues, and the trainee was able to reflect on her own sensitivity to the effect of illness on family life, arising out of a personal experience with a chronically ill parent.

Less traumatic but nevertheless stressful incidents may arise through disruption of the group setting (for example, through abrupt changes in the group room imposed by the institution hosting the group or through an assault on the group's boundary). Many and varied are the ways in which groups can be encroached upon to render them less effective as containers. An important ingredient of supervision throughout the training is the emphasis on 'dynamic administration', another core concept of group analysis which refers to the necessity for the group conductor to attend assiduously to all the details that surround the establishment of the group setting. These include selecting and preparing the group members for the group, structuring the group in time and place, and ensuring that communications taking place outside the group are ultimately woven into the dynamic context of the group itself and used to advance the therapeutic process.

When a crisis or shock does occur, the supervision group holds the trainee in a supportive way, much as a therapeutic group would, and provides the necessary space to reflect on the event. Appropriate therapeutic interventions are jointly rehearsed and the trainee is helped to understand that such occurrences are an inevitable part of therapy, and that the therapeutic group carries within itself the potential for working through and repairing the process.

SUPERVISION BEYOND THE TRAINING CONTEXT

Trainees often come to experience supervision as a necessary concomitant of therapeutic practice. Once the training has been completed and the trainee emerges into the hurly-burly of professional life, the loss of supervision is felt with a pang of uncertainty, even a feeling of deprivation. In practice, very few group-analytic therapists are able to build into their professional activities a slot for supervision. Indeed, it is an open question whether supervision should be construed as an essential element of the work routine, or a luxury for which few can afford either the time or the money and which belongs indispensably to the student role.

For more experienced therapists, the term 'supervision' itself feels uncomfortable. The notion of being looked at from above is less appropriate amongst trained peers than it is within a training context, and it would be good if some other term (perhaps 'paravision' – looking at one's work alongside another person) could gain currency. But leaving aside the problem of jargon, it would seem that those therapists who are able to gather together with a few of their colleagues and meet regularly to discuss their groups and exchange ideas, are few and far between but fortunate indeed. Group analysis rests on the assumption that interpersonal disturbance comes about through isolation. The corollary of this is that a group which fosters open communication provides an antidote to isolation. If this is true of therapeutic groups, it should be true of groups in which fellow therapists contemplate their work together.

Chapter 2

A trainee's view of supervision

Martyn Corbett

First I say this: you have seen
the strange birds, have you not, that sometimes
rest upon our river in winter?
Let them cause you to think well then of the storms
that drive many to shelter. These things
do not happen without reason.
     (William Carlos Williams, 'Gulls', 1988)[1]

Trainees on the Qualifying Course at the Institute of Group Analysis have to locate themselves in a variety of settings. There is the group of trainees admitted in the same year, with whom they are taught; the small therapy group, attended twice a week before, throughout and, often, after completing other requirements of the course; a weekly supervision group at the Institute; and, in my case, a further weekly supervision group at the NHS Hospital, St Bartholomew's, where I put together and started my training group. So it was that I brought my training group to two supervision groups, to two women supervisors.

Being supervised weekly on the same group in two supervision groups was demanding at times, just as I had been told. It obliged me to work hard at the idea of supervision as well as on what was happening for me in each of the supervision groups. I can now say it gave me a privileged opportunity to do both those things.

My supervision group at the IGA was made up of colleagues who were my contemporaries on the Qualifying Course: we were two women and two men. As the supervisor, a highly-experienced group analyst, was a woman, the men felt significantly outnumbered at times. The membership of the group was constant throughout the training. There was considerable diversity in the backgrounds of this group's members and in their experiences with their groups. What we could share, especially, were anxieties about the survival of our groups, as well as some of our fears for our own survival as conductors and trainees. Although two of the groups that we were concerned with had begun before the establishment of this supervision group, all our groups often seemed to me to be at a similar stage as they manifested there. None of my colleagues had weekly group supervision in the institutional setting in which they met their groups, as I did, and this stirred up feelings in the group that took some time for us to get round to confronting. Also, the meetings of my weekly supervision group elsewhere were not confined to the Institute's academic terms.

At the NHS Hospital, I became a member of a mature supervision group, made up largely of Qualifying Course students from the IGA at different stages of their training, along with qualified group analysts of varying experience. The supervisor was, again, a woman, a highly experienced group analyst. She was director of the psychotherapy unit and the consultant who referred patients for psychotherapy. Trainees in group work at the hospital were also encouraged to take on individual patients and to join an established supervision group in the unit with another highly experienced supervisor, again a woman. This additional training experience for me at the hospital had also to find a place in the dynamic of my supervision group at the Institute.

My training year group at the Institute found little opportunity to explore its own dynamic and I am not sure about the meaning of that. Difficulties about belonging presented themselves to me most explicitly in the two supervision groups to which I brought my training group. Evidently, the group where I received my personal psychotherapy featured significantly, too, but my group analyst was a man and my transference to him was, not discounting its inevitable vicissitudes, positive. Finally, it is worth mentioning that while the Institute of Group Analysis has a Hampstead address, the hospital I approached and which granted me the opportunity to carry out my required period of observation of a psychiatric ward, Hackney Hospital, my home, and the hospital in which I met my training group, and was supervised, were all in East London. The split with which I was to struggle in my supervision groups also had its social dimension.

During my training I was supervised in groups and I am now a member of a private partnership, one of whose attractions for me was that all its members meet weekly for supervision in groups. In my NHS work I continue in the group supervision or receive supervision with my co-facilitator in staff support work. My experience of individual supervision is limited to those few occasions when, by chance circumstance,

I have found myself alone with my supervisor. I have sought supervision in an individual setting once, on the advice of a supervisor I meet in a group setting. I had experienced uncontrollably strong affect when bringing a very damaged and depressed woman patient to supervision and was counselled to see someone who knew me well. I asked my former group analyst if he would see me and he very quickly found a time for me. During that session (and we started off not knowing if it was to be the first of a series), it became clear that I had found a mirror in my patient's grief of my own mourning for the therapy group I had left sooner than I wanted, on account of pressing practical circumstances. My turning to my analyst for further supervision had been at the behest of the unconscious that I touch that base once more. With that group strengthened inside me again, it did not seem to either my analyst or me that it was necessary for me to attend further, on this occasion. I took away again his familiar injunction to trust the unconscious and returned to my supervision group, and my work, renewed.

It is evident that in me the preference for the group setting, professionally and personally, goes very deep. In the episode above, the intimate exchange between these parts of my life is characteristic of my experience. In other, chance, experiences of being supervised alone by a supervisor whom I regularly meet in a group setting, I have noted that my transference grows more powerful, and the feeling of such encounters has sometimes been closer to that of the alliance with the analyst than that of the collaboration with the supervisor in the supervision group. For me, the advantage of the supervision group is that the transference, and also counter-transferential elements, occur in relation to more than that one object, the supervisor. What I bring from my work begins its analysis as its parts seek various objects. This is particularly evident in the supervision of group work, where the therapy group is recreated in the supervision group, and work on the group-as-a-whole, as well as on individual members, is facilitated.

The split, with which my two supervision groups during training put me in touch, appeared first in terms of how I experienced myself in each of them. In one I felt valued, in the other I felt a less secure sense of belonging. There were times, also, when the transference went the other way, but the predominant tone of my experience was that I belonged in my supervision group at the hospital and I could not find a settled place in my group at the Institute. What was also notable was that, whatever alternation might occur, there was barely a moment when I felt I belonged in both, although there were times when I felt I belonged in neither. Shortly before the closing of my group at the Institute, this pattern of fluctuations gave way and some critical restoration of what had been split was brought about in me by group process in supervision and personal therapy.

The damaged, depressed mother was very present in the founding membership of my training group. The men brought their mothers: one was a drug-abuser who had probably committed suicide; another left her son alone in the house at night and the little boy walked the streets in his pyjamas, looking for her. The women in the group were troubled mothers: one had left her children in the father's care when the marriage broke up; another had had a pregnancy terminated not long before entering the group and another termination whilst in the group. The women also brought their own mothers: one had left her children in the father's care when the daughter was in her early adolescence and was now about to leave the country to reside elsewhere; another was too preoccupied with her relationship with her depressed husband, and with her own work, to give her daughter, an only child, the loving, maternal attention the internal girl still longed for.

The young group was unstable and members left abruptly, not having found sufficiently good mothering in the group for a process of separation to be available to them. I was aware that the wholeness of the group and the wholeness of the conductor had a profound connection, and that the deficiency in the group mirrored my own deficiency, but it was the death of a male group member's father that provided the door into a fuller realisation of what was at issue. Jim's father died a couple of weeks before one of the group's breaks. Jim stopped coming to the group without saying why and did not attend again until after the group returned from the break. I was baffled, disheartened and annoyed by his disappearance. I hoped for his return and in that was supported by my supervision groups. I put that hope in the service of the group. When Jim did return to tell us of his father's death, he said that he had 'lived with him all his life without ever getting to know him'. He castigated his mother for what he saw as her hypocrisy in kissing the dying father on the lips: 'We don't do that!' My bafflement, anger and dispiritedness, it then seemed likely, had been counter-transferential, at least in part.

In both my supervision groups I felt withdrawn and a failure as a group conductor. I had difficulty in writing up my group and avoided presenting it in supervision when I could. When I took my depression to my therapy group, one member said he was surprised at my deep doubt about myself as a trainee. He was confident in me. Something stirred in me and after the next meeting of my training group I obliged myself to sit down and write it up that evening, as soon as I got home. My writing emerged as an account of my depression in the group. The conductor of a group is a member of the group as well as its conductor but I was recording myself, I found, primarily as a member only.

I left my desk to tidy my room, acting out my struggle with my chaos. I was led by my unconscious to a photograph of my parents' wedding group. I was close to Jim's perplexity and anger about his parents, if not consciously so. In the wedding photograph I saw my parents and both their families. I was astounded to see my supervisors at the IGA and at the hospital in that large group, also, it seemed. It became clearer why I had had such difficulty retaining what happened in the group, what was said to me in supervision. I was the baby in the presence of the bad breast and I was feeding listlessly, irritably. My transference to my IGA supervision group had been from my mother's family, where powerful, erratic women tended to combine to devalue the men. My transference to my hospital group had been to my father's family, which tended to idealise itself as a family of dignified men and virtuous women. My mother had been too preoccupied with her mother and sisters to turn her face to me with the absorption the baby required. My father's sister, with no child of her own, had loved me as my father's son and as she loved my father. The conditions for my depression, and the split which under-pinned it, had been constructed in a history of family groups in which my birth was only one of the comparatively more recent events.

My journey to such understanding had been resourced by my experi-ence in my therapy group where I had found, not only in the conductor, a father for whom my envy could be resolved into emulation. I had had to struggle in my supervision groups with unresolved conflicts about the mother that my group brought so painfully. I had resonated un-consciously to what the group brought and the group's fragility was a mirror of my own. The conductors have survived their own dreaded catastrophes and it is that knowledge of survival and restoration and the hope for further survivals that they put at the service of the group. I was no longer the angry impediment to the good-enough mother in the group that I had been. In time, for considerable work was still to be done, I was able to express my gratitude to both supervisors and the supervision groups for holding me through this turmoil.

As for my group, it has become a far safer, more nurturing environ-ment. It has experienced its first truly sad and happy ending when Arthur, the boy in pyjamas, gave notice of his intent and left some months later. Jean left to have her baby when she was pregnant again and wrote to the group of 'a certain calm space' in her life, afterwards. Helen took maternity leave to bear her Mary, returned and now we have her growing infant brought into the group's work. Ann, whom I had seen in another setting some time before, brought her newly born Joshua to our interview before she joined the group and it was in his presence that we agreed arrangements. Anger is more freely expressed and members of the group now swear without apologising. The group talks about its sexuality with less constraint and with keener analysis.

My experience in groups during my training as a group analyst was evidently invaluable to me. In my therapy group I worked to repair the father and in another group member I encountered, in the transference, the brother who never existed but whose superior nature I feared would finally eclipse me in my parents' eyes. He was a fellow trainee at the Institute. The group member who encouraged me when I most needed it was, in the transference, my late Uncle Fred, my father's brother, who had experienced early deprivation comparable with what my fellow analysand was struggling with. In my IGA group supervision, in the transference, I encountered not only my dangerous mother but some of her sisters, my aunts with children of their own who came first in their concern. I had some difficulty in relating to my colleagues' groups, my sets of cousins, as I envied them. In my hospital supervision, I encountered not only my aunt, my good mother, in the transference, but also the authoritarian, paternalistic culture of my father's family: it was there I met the shadow therapist in me, severe and moralistic. I began to learn to accept and negotiate with him. My infant training group experienced early needs that I recreated in my supervision groups with the inflection of my own unresolved early experiences.

The supervision group provides a theatre in which the conductors' experience of the drama of their groups may be recreated and analysed. For trainee conductors, because of the variety of objects the group provides, it is the place where interwoven transferential strands may be teased apart and where they can learn to tolerate, and contemplate as material essential to their work, the volley of projections to which they are especially exposed as conductor. In learning also to disengage the identificatory dimension in this experience, the trainee conductors come to understand their groups and themselves to a mutual advantage which is at the core of their professional training.

Close to the end of a late paper, S. H. Foulkes (Foulkes 1974: 280) wrote: 'We are involved far more than we usually know; too much so, perhaps.' During my training at the Institute of Group Analysis I had experience of the force of this dictum, in the group supervision of my work with my group. What I have taken away is that the supervision group can offer a safe place in which to explore my involvement in my group work and, just as important, to own my continuing frequent ignorance of the sort, intensity and history of my involvement. My involvement with my supervision group is an image of my involvement as conductor with my therapeutic group. My supervision group offers me the opportunity to contemplate that image in a professional setting where my effectiveness and my own well-being come together, in the common, collaborative, professional pursuit, with my colleagues, in the service of my group-analytic group. It was a colleague who had given me an essential synopsis of the supervision experience that might lie ahead of me in the training, and my supervisors and colleagues who made it possible for it to work out for me in the way it did. It became the very worthwhile experience I had been told was available.

As a final illustration of how the supervision group is a place where matrix overlaps matrix, one of my supervisors told me very recently that there was a marked similarity, in one particular, between our family histories. We agreed that this must have contributed beneficially to the work I was able to do in her supervision group, as part of my professional training and in the service of my training group.

NOTE

1   *William Carlos Williams: Collected Poems, 1909–1939. Vol I.* © 1938 New Directions Publishing Corp. Reprinted by permission of New Directions.

REFERENCES

Foulkes, S. A. (1974) 'My philosophy in psychotherapy', *Journal of Contemporary Psychotherapy* 6: 280 [Reprinted in *Selected Papers*, London: Karnac Books, 1990].

Williams, William Carlos (1988) 'Gulls', in A. W. Litz and C. J. MacGowan (eds) *Collected Poems*, Manchester: Carcanet Press Ltd.

Chapter 3

Simultaneous supervision and personal analysis

Lisbeth E. Hearst
Rachel Brown

Part I Supervisor

Lisbeth E. Hearst

In the training of group analysts, the Institute of Group Analysis
(London) has developed a triadic structure in which the personal
analysis, the supervision, and the teaching proceed simultaneously. The
co-ordinating of the three building blocks of the training to proceed in
unison aims at imparting meaning and significance to the learning
process; it avoids fragmentation and a false division between the experience of the personal analysis, the supervision, and the theory, in this
manner facilitating personal and professional growth and authenticity
(Kernberg 1985).

This triadic structure exposes the trainee throughout the training to
the interactions and emotional influences of three groups: the analytic
therapy group, the supervision group, and the theory seminar group.
There is yet another constellation of groups that shapes the experience
of the trainee: the trainee's own therapy group, the training group he or
she is conducting, and the supervision group. Their continuous
interaction and overlap make considerable emotional and intellectual
demands on the trainee, who must go in and out of states of functioning
and perceiving in quick succession and also interact with and respond to
the group analyst, the supervisor, and the teachers of theory.

The task of maintaining clear, yet creative, boundaries between
therapy and supervision falls in the first place to the analyst and the
supervisor (Sharpe and Blackwell 1987). If sensitively handled, these
interactive and multiple relationships can bring about a change and
growth-inducing process which ultimately enhances the trainee's

conscious and unconscious responsiveness to both patients and groups: in the therapy group, the trainee/patient experiences deep self-realisation; in the supervision group, it should emerge how far these realisations have clinical value for the trainee's work as a group analyst; in the theory group, structures and concepts are given flesh and blood by self-realisations and their clinical application.

But there are also potential pitfalls to this structure, which can cause trauma and do harm to trainees at a time of heightened vulnerability in their personal and professional development (Fuller 1992). Intellectual or emotional discord between the group analyst and the supervisor, especially when they are unconscious and therefore unacknowledged, place the trainee in an emotional dilemma and can induce the very splitting processes which the unified training scheme is designed to avoid. In the analytic group, the trainee is also a full member-patient who partakes in the regressive, transferential and projective processes which constitute much of the therapy. These must be experienced and worked through unhindered by the complications of another trans-ference relationship which can easily occur in the supervision situation: that of the benevolent or stern, approving or disapproving, father-mother-teacher of early relationships. Unconscious or conscious rivalry or animosity between the analyst and the supervisor have to be detected and resolved so as not to involve the trainee emotionally or cognitively in it. The greatly enlarged field of the training situation in which the multiple transference unfolds can include the training institute itself (Hearst and Sharpe 1991). Under such conditions there is ample oppor-tunity for splitting into all-good and all-bad, caring and uncaring, being held and being abandoned, between the therapy group, the group analyst, the supervisor, the supervision group and the training course itself. The emergence of these powerful emotions, if detected and addressed, can be of vitally important therapeutic significance and increase the efficacy of the therapy and the supervision.

A woman started the first supervision session after the long summer break by telling the supervision group of a traumatic start of her training group after the summer break: the composition of her carefully constructed group had been changed drastically by outside intervention on the part of the institution in which the group was conducted. She had come into the first session without having been told that there would be two new patients in her group. The old group members were angry and shaken in their trust in her. She herself was unsure of her next step: to accept the new members or to ask them to leave. If she did, would this be injurious to them? If not, would it be injurious to her group, who had been working well before the break? It had been an awful situation. Fortunately, she told the supervision group, she had been able to talk about it in her own therapy group.

The case was now eagerly discussed by the supervision group and she was confirmed in her decision to weather the storm and accept the newcomers. However, the supervisor (a woman) was left with a nagging feeling that something vital had remained unmentioned and unexplored. She asked the supervisee why, since this crisis had taken place before the first supervision session of the term, she had not availed herself of the arrangement made for breaks: namely that the supervisees could phone the supervisor at home when an urgent or upsetting problem occurred in their training groups. The supervisee became thoughtful and after a while said she thought it was because she did not want to show herself as needy to the supervisor. She added that she had had the feeling that the supervisor was overburdened with work.

Once pronounced, it became clear to everyone in the supervision group that they were in the presence not of a realistic appraisal of the situation but of a transference distortion. The supervisee herself almost immediately found the key to her perception and feelings: she had unconsciously established the relationship with the supervisor which she had had with her sick mother in childhood. This had not at the time emerged in her analytic group, possibly because the conductor was a man and the group did not lend itself to this transference. It was not taken further in supervision, but directed to the therapy group for exploration. The emergence of this transference relationship, for which there had been a previous, but unclear, indication, cleared the supervision relationship from a transference distortion and greatly helped the supervisee to use the supervision fully and realistically.

The reverse process, in this case one in which the repression of rage and intolerable anxiety in the therapy group surfaces, unconsciously expressed, in the supervision group, can be seen in the following vignette:

In a supervision group which had worked together for a considerable time, it was the turn of one supervisee to report on his training group, which he had been conducting sensitively and capably for eighteen months. He reported that all was well with the group; it was working on deep levels, and there was good empathy and support for one another in the group, which enabled the group members to make progress also in their lives outside the group. He gave as an example 'a happy arrangement' in which a group member had offered another member a temporary home and a computer, to enable him to complete a thesis due in a course of studies. The two group members would share the home till the work was done, and they would come to the group sessions together in the car of one of the two, to the convenience of them both. The supervisee was obviously pleased with this arrangement and concluded his report.

There was consternation in the supervision group. Could their colleague not see that he was allowing the carefully constructed and maintained setting – that of a stranger group in which the participants had no social connections with one another outside the group – to be offended against? This was an acting-out, but of what? Most puzzling was the unquestioning acceptance of this behaviour by their hitherto sensitive and capable colleague. When this was addressed, he told the group that it so happened that in his own therapy group he found himself with someone he worked with; if he could put up with this, surely his patient could, too? The supervision group inquired what he felt about this unusual situation, and how it had come about.

Further exploration revealed that below his apparent acceptance of a most difficult situation beyond his control, there was suppressed and unacknowledged rage and disappointment with his much loved and admired therapist and his group. He, the trainee, was taught one thing and had to submit to its opposite. At this point, the supervisor suggested that he took it back to his therapy group now that he was aware of his real feelings about the situation. This was done, and the trainee reported to the supervision group that much had been resolved for him and the therapy group subsequently.

The supervision group did not concern itself with the outcome: this belonged strictly to the supervisee's therapy group. What belonged to the supervision group was the trainee's insight into his patients' behaviour, which was possible only when the projections had been taken back where they belonged, that is, to the trainee and his therapy group. The trainee had been 'using' his patients and his training group to defend against unbearable rage and disappointment with his own therapist and his own therapy group. While uncovering this process, the supervision group and the supervisor had kept the boundary between the two functions – supervision and therapy – by using what emerged in supervision only in the service of comprehending the dynamic processes in the training group. This was impossible as long as the collusion on the part of the trainee remained unconscious.

The close proximity of the training components – the analysis, the supervision, the theory teaching – means that there is also a close proximity of the group analysts involved in the training: they are colleagues, and they meet frequently in their work in the Institute and on the training course. Furthermore, each one of them at times fills more than one function – often all three, albeit with different groups. This makes it all the more important to beware of a temporary role confusion or competitiveness. If these occur they must be reflected and resolved, lest they intrude on the trainee and turn a potentially enabling and therapeutic training situation into destructive acting-out. A space for such interchange is needed, but at the same time, utmost confidentiality with regard to the trainee must be maintained, especially concerning all that happens in the analytic group. This can be achieved if the exchange between group analyst, supervisor and teachers concerns their own feelings and thoughts evoked by the training activities, rather than those of the trainee. It is a delicate situation which requires discipline, and, above all, mutual appreciation of and trust in one's colleagues and the training institute.

The fact that the supervision takes place not in a one-to-one relationship but in a group makes it easier to detect, scrutinise and remedy rivalry, competitiveness and role confusion. In a sense it is the entire supervision group that is the supervisor, and it possesses discernment and insights which transcend the insights of its individual members, including those of the supervisor. This is clearly noticeable when one reflects on the various supervision groups one is engaged in. In each group, the supervisor's function is subtly different, evoked by and adjusted to the supervision group itself. It is also noticeable when trainees leave the supervision group at the end of their training and new ones enter in a slow-open pattern which mirrors the pattern of the therapy groups. Each new member subtly influences and changes the supervision group through his or her personality, manner of group conducting, strength, weaknesses and needs.

In a supervision group two members, a man and a woman, had left at the end of their training, and two new trainees were entering it. One was at the beginning of the training, the other had another year ahead of her and had joined the group because her old one had closed. (The slow-open pattern makes this necessary at times.) There was a sense of loss in the supervision group, even a degree of mourning: the old group had functioned so well; there had been trust and intimacy in the group, and members had felt free to expose their weaknesses, admit to uncertainty, not-knowing, mistakes. In fact, the group and its supervisor had experienced their supervision sessions as wholly satisfactory. There was a weariness in the group at having 'to start all over again', to adjust to the newcomers, to win trust and establish the intimacy the work requires.

The newcomer to the training as well as to the supervision group posed less of a challenge. The 'older ones' had always enjoyed sharing their expertise in the manner of older siblings. They were also aware of having a second chance to work through earlier problem situations through the presentations of the new trainee conductor. The problem seemed to be the other newcomer, who was far from being a beginner. She was withdrawn and contributed relatively little to the work of the others, though she presented her own training group clearly and interestingly and engaged the supervision group well in discussion and reflection of the dynamics of her group and patients.

The supervisor experienced a reluctance on the part of the newcomer to engage with her, and at times something akin to hostility. Altogether, the supervision group was a very different place now; some of the openness and trust had gone. Of course, she thought, trust takes time to develop and cannot be taken for granted in supervision: one did, after all, make oneself vulnerable by presenting one's group-conducting with all its potential shortcomings, missed opportunities and mistakes. However, she felt there was more to it than that, and she started the session by presenting her impression of the change of atmosphere in the group and invited the members to comment on this. This was taken up with obvious relief and the whole session was devoted to speaking frankly about feelings of loss and a reluctance to engage with the newcomers.

What also emerged was that though the first-year student was happy with his placement, the experienced trainee whose group had been closed felt 'like a refugee' who had lost her family. She thought her new supervisor did not recognise and value her expertise and was 'talking down' to her. This, she thought, prevented the supervision group from appreciating her contributions. The supervisor was puzzled by this: she had been appreciative of the work of this trainee, and had not, she thought, in any way devalued her. Was she, the supervisor, unconsciously in competition with the previous supervisor, and therefore needed to make the newcomer 'start all over again'? She was in no way aware of such feelings, but it was just possible! The supervision group did not analyse the feelings and thoughts offered; rather, they were voiced and accepted. In the following session the usual work proceeded, and the atmosphere was once more one of warmth, engagement and interest in one another and in one another's group work.

Supervision in the training of group analysts is an integral and important part of the training. It is therefore paramount that the supervision group, like the therapy group, be kept in optimal condition to enable it to fulfil its functions. By proceeding with its work parallel to and in unison with the therapy group, a mutual emotional and cognitive interaction is engendered which makes the training a holistic learning and growth experience.

REFERENCES – PART I

Foulkes, S.H. (1964) *Therapeutic Group Analysis*, London: George Allen & Unwin.

Fuller, V.G. (1992) 'Group disequilibrium: risk factor or agent of change?', Unpublished.

Hearst, L.E. and Sharpe, M. (1991) 'Training for and trainees in group analysis', p. 150 in J. Roberts and M. Pines (eds) *The Practice of Group Analysis*, London: Routledge.

Kernberg, O.F. (1985) 'Organisational problems of psychoanalytic education', paper presented at a Conference on Idealisation Transference and Authoritarian Pressure in Psychoanalytic Education, Columbia University, New York, 5 February.

Sharpe, M. and Blackwell, D. (1987) 'Creative supervision through student involvement', *Group Analysis* 20(3): 203.

Part II Supervisee/analysand

Rachel Brown

In attempting to write something about my experience as supervisee and analysand, I have been preoccupied with the relationship between myself as a private individual and myself as a professional, working woman.

I came to the group-analytic training from medicine and psychiatry, aware that both had made demands on me. Although I felt at home in my profession and took comfort and pride from it, I knew that it had limitations, both at a professional and a personal level. Isabel Menzies Lyth (Lyth 1988: 63) has written about the social defence system of nursing within an NHS hospital: 'The characteristic feature of the social defence system, as we have described it, is its orientation to helping the individual avoid the experience of anxiety, guilt, doubt and uncertainty'. Although the subtleties of the defences are different, a similar system operates in medicine, ensuring that doctors are protected from the anxiety created in their work by, for example, strict hierarchies, the rapid rotation of junior staff, and the characterisation of patients by diagnosis.

On a personal level, the place of my work in my life, and the particular limitations it has presented me with, are, of course, hopelessly intertwined with the nature of the person I am, and with my history. Once, soon after I first started any sort of therapy, I dreamed that I was walking through a prison, and people were calling out, 'Dr Brown, Dr Brown'. I got to the centre of the prison, and said, 'No, I'm not Dr Brown. I'm Brown'. My application for the Qualifying Course, some years later, was, therefore, inevitably both a professional development and a personal step. When I was asked how it would be if my application were turned down, I did not talk about the limitations it would pose to me in my professional life. I said, feeling very anxious, that it would be as if a limb were amputated.

I came to the training, therefore, wishing (among other things) for an opportunity to explore further the links between private and professional life. Theoretically, group analysis recognised the importance of the relationship between the internal world described by psychoanalysis, and the external world described by sociology and systems theory. Practically, the training brought the relationship of internal to external world to life with the movement from patient, to supervisee, to pupil within the space of a few hours, and, of necessity, brought into sharp focus the different requirements of each activity. Seminars, the large group, discussions with the co-ordinator of training, and with contemporaries provided an opportunity to become aware of the culture and structures of the institution of group analysis, of its external relationships and of its ancestors. Being a patient meant the opportunity for the exploration and exposure of an internal world, and of parts of oneself which have been hidden even from oneself in a setting where there is permission to be suspicious of reticence – indeed, where 'there is no hiding place' (Okeke 1993). In supervision there was an awareness, at one and the same time, of the external world of work, and the maintenance of an essential privacy. There was a concern for the public encounter in the work setting, and a parallel awareness of the possibility that the state of mind of the therapist might impinge on the ability to work. Supervision supported the maintenance of an essential privacy, and of a hidden self, in order to do professional work. As Foulkes put it, the therapeutic attitude rests on 'his refusal to contribute more than a minimum of personal, private information . . . to be as little as possible involved as a private person' (Foulkes 1984: 160).

Foulkes was also clear, however, that the therapeutic attitude necessitates emotional involvement in the group and rests on the personality and empathy of the therapist, and 'has to be genuine and cannot be faked or adopted' (Foulkes 1984: 179). I think that groups are particularly demanding of honesty on the part of the therapist, because of the visibility of the body, in which the true self in Winnicott's terms 'comes from the aliveness of the heart's action and breathing' (Winnicott 1965: 148). Face to face with the patient, or face to face with a group as a patient, I am essentially the same person, and will become only the student, the patient, the supervisee and the group analyst that I can become.

Some time ago, a colleague, Kajetan Kasinski, and I wrote about supervision:

> If the session between therapist and patient can be thought of as a painting, then recording the session afterwards is like doing a sketch of the painting, and presenting the session in supervision is doing a sketch of the sketch. . . . To make good use of the supervision, the supervisee becomes aware that each supervisor is more familiar with sketches in different mediums, and that to make optimum use of the supervision the sketch should be in the appropriate one, e.g. one supervisor understands best two or three lines in finely drawn ink, another a finger painting. This then affects the painting (that is, the session), in that the paintings become those most easily sketched in a particular material – that is adapted for ease of sketching.
>
> (Brown and Kasinski 1985)

Of course, it is more complicated than this because, as patient, therapist and supervisee, I am at the same time painted, painter and painting, but I hope the analogy illustrates some of the parallel experiences of supervisee and analysand.

First, the different activities as a trainee are separate, but necessarily related, in the sense that works of art by the same artist are the same and related, even though they are in different mediums, in the style of different schools, or assisted by different teachers.

Second, the most important aspects of the experience of supervision and analysis are not simply verbal and theoretical. This was so for me, even though, as a clever child I spoke and wrote early. It is difficult to express this experience in an account – inevitably for a book – in words. For a time, a personal loss rendered me a silent patient within my group, although I continued to be there, and, in retrospect, I value that experience and the group's patience greatly. My patients were never told in words why I was briefly absent, although I am sure that my work was affected for many weeks. Supervision became a sort of crossroads where I had to speak of the relationship between my sadness and my work. I fancy that the presence of women (I had both a female analyst and supervisor) facilitated the process of experiencing and speaking the unspeakable.

Third, the activities of a trainee are idiosyncratic and creative. Each trainee comes to group analysis 'in possession of his own personality, his very unique configuration of being (what I term an idiom) that has never really changed in itself' (Bollas 1989: 2), looking for answers: '. . . as I imagine myself in the future, working in these areas, which one do I feel to be the evolution of my idiom? Where shall I find experiences of myself?' (ibid.: 42).

I think passionately that analysis and supervision are profoundly unhelpful when, rather than allowing an educated and informed acquaintance with a body of knowledge, they constitute only the learning of concepts and the imposition of rules. At its best, a training like ours can allow the development of analysts in relationship to the existing members of the IGA, not in imitation of them. The complaints and demands we trainees directed at the institution were legitimate, I believe, because creative development requires a creative environment like that required for the development of a creative child: '. . . a state of eager aliveness in two people, the infant with the potential for life and the mother alive inside herself and tuning in to the emerging infant' (Balint 1993: 102). In looking ahead to my professional life, I would use Balint's words again to refer to analyst as to author, to action and experience as to words, and to groups as to the individual: 'The writer cannot use words passively accepted from someone else, which to him are meaningless. He must create his own, but again, they arise in relation to another person' (Balint 1993: 103).

REFERENCES – PART II

Balint, E. (1993) 'Creative life', Chapter 8 in J. Mitchell and M. Parsons (eds) *Before I was I: Psychoanalysis and the Imagination*, London: Free Association Books.

Bollas, C. (1989) *Forces of Destiny: Psychoanalysis and Human Idiom*, London: Free Association Books.

Brown, R.M.A. and Kasinski, K. (1985) Unpublished communication.

Foulkes, S.H. (1984) *Therapeutic Group Analysis*, London: Karnac Books.

Lyth, I.M. (1988) 'The functioning of social systems as a defence against anxiety', in I.M. Lyth *Containing Anxiety in Institutions, Selected Essays*, London: Free Association Books.

Okeke, A.-O. (1993) 'Conflict in the search for an "Individual Self"', *Group Analysis* 26(3).

Winnicott, D. (1960) 'Ego distortion in terms of true and false self', in D. Winnicott (1965) *The Maturational Processes and the Facilitating Environment: Studies in the Theory of Emotional Development*, London: The Hogarth Press and the Institute of Psycho-Analysis.

Chapter 4

Presenting groups effectively

Meg Sharpe

As a supervisor, I operate most frequently within the umbrella scheme of the Institute of Group Analysis, but I have my own individual ideas on session design, which are illustrated here. Influences in my own career have inevitably coloured my approach. Among these I would single out:

- Drama school, which helped me to identify with different characters, to try to think and feel a way into someone else's skin.
- Sociological research, which taught me the importance of detail and report writing.
- Music therapy, which trained me to listen, to observe, to wait, to experience, to be unknowing, to allow for the unexpected.
- Experiences with teachers, students, patients, past and present.

A supervisor's own presentation is also of extreme importance; its mood can be contagious. Dull, jaded, overworked teachers influence the trainees much more than may be realised: they may infect both the supervision and the patient groups. One can supervise joyfully or boringly.

In developing presentation skills my general approach is non-didactic and developmental. It starts with methods and material that the students choose and then moves on to frame these into disciplines which may make them more useful. For example, an initial unstructured series of presentations by students enables them at least to see how to organise material and the need to organise it. I prefer to let them present in their own individual ways, and to experiment with their own reporting ideas before attempting to refine and develop these. The intention is not to provide entertainment for the supervision group; both the group and the supervisor need to know what is going on in the patient group and the therapist's perception of the process.

From the students' point of view, a main component of learning how to conduct is to be able to understand, to translate into interventions what is going on in their groups, and to evaluate and draw conclusions from the data. In addition they also have to increase personal knowledge about themselves – their nervous habits, patterns of speech, and uses of language which may get in the way and inhibit the performance of their groups. They need to learn about their own message transmission as well as transmissions from the group. It can be difficult to convince students that their mannerisms and body language may impede or obstruct, and this is where use of a video can be useful. The result is often surprising and may help the presenter to acknowledge quirks such as excessive fidgeting, or gestures which could be distracting. It is helpful to be comfortable in 'one's own skin'. The intention is not to produce therapists who are static, fixed and unnatural in their manner, but to encourage them to reflect, to be aware that some mannerisms may and do intrude on the group process.

How to prepare and present reports is an art in itself and people's personalities fit different styles: the obsessional will slog away and slog away and work it out; others need random notes, ideas on bits of paper in back pockets, conversations with colleagues which register in their minds, they carry it all around with them. Eventually they have to say it or write it down and the way they get there depends very much on their attention span. Some people simply cannot sit down and write at length – all they can do is dictate into a recorder, hand it to a secretary, get a draft, revise the draft, and keep sending it back until they think it is all right. This is expensive in time, but often produces good material which may transmit as very spontaneous.

Setting a high professional standard is part of the task also, and the way a supervisor plans and prepares sessions, holds boundaries, etc., will reverberate through the supervision group. If supervisors use the group's power and control rather than their own, then the students are more likely to present an honest account of events in their groups rather than saying what it is thought a 'controlling' supervisor might want to hear. What is clear is that students reveal how they are as therapists by the way they present, as the following examples illustrate:

> Y, a sincere thoughtful person, always presented a surface, shallow account of group 'happenings'. What became evident in the ensuing discussion was that she was conducting a 'supportive' group rather than an analytic one because of personal anxieties that needed to be addressed both in the supervision group and in detail in her therapy.

J presented a dazzling account of a fast-moving, action-packed group that left the supervision group stunned. It moved so rapidly that there was no space for reflection – one could only speculate that his group was infected by his energetic virtuosity, but it was not necessarily indicative of where the members were at individually or collectively. He needed to calm down and contain his own anxiety without losing his enthusiasm.

M exhibited much anxiety in her presentations halfway through the winter term. Nothing in the group events could account for this. She was invited to share what was troubling her at a personal disclosure level, if she wished. She then related that this evening group was conducted in an isolated part of an old hospital – she had to rearrange the chairs and lock up the room afterwards and walk through long empty corridors. She felt unsafe and frightened and now that winter was approaching, she hated going there. She felt she had no right to question the arrangements as she was a 'guest' therapist in that setting. The supervision group enabled her to face and change the reality problem so that she could work more comfortably.

Reflections from the supervision group on the style of these presentations proved helpful.

Another aim of training in presentation is to help students to remember, to listen and to observe. To develop their memories students need not only to report at intervals about their clinical work, but to discover methods of remembering that can aid them in the future when they become practitioners with no reporting obligations. How does one remember? There are many modes:

- Pictorially   who sat where;
- Emotionally   how the therapist feels entering the room/how the group feels;
- Factually   by main themes;
- Incidentally   by particular events, like a film unwinding, or the synopsis of a book;
- Chronologically   with a factual account rather like a shopping list.

As for refining the art of listening, how attentive are the students to each other's presentations? Pointing out distracting behaviour at supervision can help here – for example, the student who is busy going through notes while someone else is presenting. Most people listen, but not very well. The meaning needs to be understood – what the words are saying, what the presenter is trying to convey. If nobody is listening, there is little point in talking. Students need to be helped to be alert and concentrated listeners, to be open to subtleties of speech and expression, to learn and listen not only to their patients' language but to their fellow supervisees' language.

Alongside this is the skill of speaking to be heard, of speaking with clarity – which can be developed by encouraging experiments with presentations.

Observation skills are extremely valuable. Therapists are encouraged to use not only their intellect and emotions, but also their vision, to use their eyes like cameras, noting fine details, variations of expressions, posture, moods, etc. Observation skills, or their absence, can be detected in presentations. Just as the analyst is trained to use the eye, so the group analyst needs to be trained to be observant and note details however small. Enid Balint (Balint 1993: 12) clearly describes this: 'The best thing an analyst can do to begin with is first to make observations and not be too worried if he cannot fit them into any particular theory'. And again, 'The central task is to observe with a free and curious mind and not to be distracted by theories and the easy solutions they may offer' (Balint 1993: 17).

I shall now examine several tested approaches to the presentations which students have found valuable in clarifying to themselves and others what is going on in their groups, and in understanding their own strengths and weaknesses as developing therapists.

The following styles of presentation will be discussed:

- Process;
- Single issue;
- Spontaneous report;
- Individual focusing;
- Kaleidoscopic approach;
- Theoretical analysis;
- Brainstorming.

PROCESS PRESENTATION

Here is a straightforward process account by a student of the nineteenth session of her once-weekly evening group, held in a psychiatric hospital. The students were asked to identify some of the group processes and the presenting conductor to recount her responses (these appear between double asterisks). Although it is lengthy I have left it largely complete because of the importance of illustrating a full range of processes and the nature of the involvement of the student presenter.

Presenter ** 'On the way to the group I was cornered by an inpatient and for the first time was late – five minutes. They were all there waiting, which was unusual. As I went through the door it was almost like crossing a barrier – the atmosphere had some kind of tension. For a moment I thought there was a stranger sitting in my group – then I realised it was R who had let his hair grow long, grown a beard, and shed his usual "Elton Lives" T-shirt for a smart pin-striped suit and immaculate white shirt. I thought some identification was going on – two of the men always wore suits – R had seen me in the local shopping precinct with my husband, who has a beard.'**

Processes identified by students

The group started in tense silence

A asked R if he had managed on his own during his two weeks away.
R said that he was OK, a bit lightheaded. Surprisingly glad to be back at work but that nothing had changed with his home situation.

Further silence

X asked if I could provide a letter for her employers as they were beginning to query the amount of time she had to have off to get here, but that would I please write the letter without mentioning the psychiatric hospital and group therapy; just please call it therapy.

Silence

Resistance

B was looking very uncomfortable.
D pushed her chair out of the group and sat staring at the floor.
B all of a sudden blurted out, 'I have to tell the group about Monday'. For the next half hour he rambled on in the most muddled way about coming to the hospital on Monday morning without really specifying anything.

D-unconscious identification with B. She has previously overdosed.

The group allowed him to go on with this but they all looked very anxious and D especially looked very detached from what was happening.

Environment affecting group	**During this half hour somebody in another room started to play operatic music very loudly. It got louder until I could not hear what was being said and had to go out and try to get the music turned down. It
Flight from anxiety and tension	was a good five minutes before I could return. When I did the group were telling one another jokes and were in complete disarray. I sat down trying very hard not to look like a disapproving school mistress, and in the end most of the laughter subsided. D and A continued to giggle.**

R: 'You are going to have to throw those two out.'

I felt I had to take a hold of the group and I said I wondered just how difficult it had been for the group to listen to B who had become so overwhelmed with the feelings provoked by the previous group that he had felt like committing suicide and had become desperate enough to seek help, and that I had seen him on Monday, after asking him to wait for an hour as I was occupied.

Silence – lengthy

X looked very anxious (his mother had committed suicide).

D angrily said she was appalled that B had to wait for an hour; she thought that if people got help when they asked for it, then all sorts of things would never happen to them – they would be prevented from collapsing.

Transference Therapist = Mother-in-law	** I said that D was very angry and the anger was relevant to her own situation.**

D: 'How dare you send B away. People never get help when they need it.'

** I asked her whether she felt that she got enough help from me.**

D said that I was always criticising her and accusing her of escaping – she did not need that kind of help but needed help to lift her mind from her problems.

** I pronounced that this was not a place to escape to, it was a place to find out why she was in difficulties.**

Threats – resistance	D replied that when she was made to look at her problems and her attempted suicide she began to think

about it; to think about it was to plan it, and to plan it was to make another attempt, which was what she really wanted anyway.

I interpreted that every time D was asked to look at herself in relation to others in the group she told them to go away, not to get too close, that to question her was to endanger her life.

D: 'Look, I have said it before, when I start to think about suicide it is like dangling a carrot in front of my nose, it is like putting a cream bun in front of a child, if you leave it there long enough I will take it.'

The group was getting very tense.

R said, 'I don't think D is really angry'.

I felt he was saying to me, 'Don't push her any further'.

S did not think D was angry but then she could not see her face.

B said he definitely picked up anger.

X thought that D was very angry with me.

Splitting

C and D opted out, pushed chairs back, looked too anxious to say or do anything and I felt that D had split the group three ways and in some way managed to be very destructive. I wanted to interpret that this was how she related to her family but I was so anxious about whether or not the group could cope with any more confrontation of D that I left it.

Counter-transference

Silence – tense

S broke the silence by asking B what actually happened. She said she was not very clear.

Catharsis

B then very clearly and with a lot of real feeling told the group how he had come to the hospital and that I had asked him to wait an hour. I then saw him; the one thing that had carried him through was that although he still felt dreadful when he left the hospital, I had said to him that I would see him Thursday night at the group. If I had said that, I must have had enough confidence in him and felt that he could cope. Although he felt completely desperate the following day it gave him enough support to carry him through.

Support   S said that surely the therapist would not have sent him away if she had thought that he would kill himself. Social workers can assess clearly whether or not people will take their own lives.

I said S was asking whether I could give her some boundaries if she felt she was going to lose control of herself.

S said that a little while ago she had felt desperate and had almost telephoned me, that I was the person she thought about because I always seemed like an anchor.

I said it seemed as if she was asking whether it was OK to come to see me outside group time if she was feeling desperate like B had felt. At this point I realised that the group had run five minutes over time, and I ended it.

The presenting student felt that this was the most difficult group she had ever sat in, she was extremely anxious, wondering whether she could hold on to it and stop it fragmenting. It was very stressful for her to wait for the next supervision, and she had thought about phoning the supervisor and getting an extra session (like B).

The supervision group commented on her style; they felt she had held the group well, that she was totally there, experiencing the atmosphere and that she had appeared to contain her anxiety. They pointed out some of the processes they had identified and discussed other ways of dealing with the outside disturbance. This presentation held the group's interest. The students listened emotionally as well as intellectually and showed empathy with the presenter. For the therapist this group was a milestone. She emerged from supervision feeling encouraged and strengthened by the response of the group.

A full account like the above is necessary from time to time in order to get a clear (or otherwise) picture of the therapist and the group at work so that technical or therapeutic errors and difficulties can be monitored and corrected.

A contrasting style of process presentation is shown in the following vignette. This is a first group session; the therapist has had some experience of conducting hospital groups already and is just beginning formal training. It does not give much detail of events or of the therapist's feelings but nevertheless the presentation illustrates the first movement of a group concerto that is beginning to take shape.

The group started off with my introducing myself and stating that this was confidential. This was followed by a long silence with people looking very restless and anxious. I broke the silence saying I wondered what the silence was about, what people were thinking about during it. G said that she was trying to think what to say to start it off and she felt very anxious – followed by one or two others expressing their anxieties about being there.

X said that he normally could chat in groups very easily but now he was struggling with himself not to get the group started. He said that he felt ill, had a sore throat and a temperature and was wondering whether to go home, or stay in the group. What he had done, in fact, was to get some antibiotics before coming to the group. I said something about the power of the group to cure him. Various remarks followed including: Why was he trying to do something different? Was that why he had got a sore throat? Why hold back if it makes you feel unhappy and your natural feeling is to join in? X recounted that when he was a six-year-old child he had to take himself to school and had never really understood why and had been cross about it; only in later life did he understand when his mother said that she had to let him do it on his own because she had to look after his sick sister who was two years younger. Then it all made sense.

There was one silent side of the room. C expressed some positive feelings towards D who said her nose was cold and her hands were cold, she felt the way to get warm was to join in. He said they should greet each other like the Eskimos do, rubbing noses. There was a lot of relieved laughter about this. C said that he felt quite interested in her. She looked rather surprised and he said that he would not be intrusive – at least the gist of what he was saying was that he was attracted by her but he was going to take it slowly.

S (a younger man with curly hair, bright blue soulful eyes) sat looking very puzzled for a long time and eventually said that he also was attracted by D and he felt some kinship with C, but also some rivalry with him. Most people then talked about not knowing what to say and feeling anxious. E anxiously said that he always looked for a friend in a situation like this, he always would look for a woman and then he would feel safer and that there was one woman in the group that in fact he felt he liked. He pointed out M. People were already bringing transference feelings from the past into this group. I found it a slow group with a lot of silences.

SINGLE ISSUE

This is a form of presentation that focuses on a special piece of behaviour, e.g. acting out, absenteeism.

First vignette

The therapist reported that she had felt fed up and angry with Jo, who kept coming late to the group and who stayed away regularly. He would miss three out of four sessions then turn up again, especially if he had received a letter from her. He had great difficulty in getting out of bed most days – was unemployed, depressed, abandoned by his family, felt worthless. The major problem was how to get him to come. Meantime the group had grappled with the issue, talked about their feelings of rejection and Jo's special position – 'the favourite', 'we all come on time', 'he gets attention because he misses', and so on.

The supervision group contributed various ideas including giving him a time limit: he must improve attendance in two months by coming regularly. They suggested the therapist was condoning acting-out: 'he's testing you', 'stop writing so many letters', 'throw him out'. The supervision group responded like the real group. It became quite clear that the student was reluctant to lay down the law. The supervisor suggested that she looked at her counter-transference. What does this behaviour mean to her, what does Jo mean? He has been abandoned and he is trying to drive the therapist to chuck him out, therefore to abandon him. She was advised to stop being a 'kind Mum' and to start exploring and interpreting what his behaviour meant, both to her and to him.

The presenter later reported that dealing with her own fears of abandonment in her personal therapy had helped her to empathise with Jo, to deal with her counter-transference, and thus to facilitate his attendance at the group, which eventually became regular.

Second vignette

A student reported that one member of his newish group brought a can of Coca-Cola with him every week. This was noted but no comment was made, either by him or anyone else in the group. Soon another member brought coffee, followed close upon by a third. At this point the student felt he should bring this issue to supervision, as he was uncertain how to deal with it. His fear was that all eight members would shortly bring drinks and croissants. He said he felt rather ashamed and that he should have dealt with this firmly in the first instance. The supervision group developed a somewhat judgemental attitude and suggested rather punitive interpretations. The supervisor pointed out that two out of five students brought drinks and sandwiches to supervision. What did they make of this? After a startled silence, the responses were reality based: 'Oh, there just isn't time to get lunch before coming', 'This isn't a therapy group'. Asked to consider the issue symbolically, they were surprised to contact their own neediness and anxiety as first-year students. The presenting student understood the significance of the event in his group and went away relieved, with some idea about how to tackle this issue analytically.

SPONTANEOUS REPORT

This involves instructing students to jettison all notes – 'putting the students on the spot'.

Students recall from memory what happened in the last group. It can often be quite revealing in terms of what is remembered and what is forgotten if the student's notes are checked later. This method encourages them to work at processing information and making some sense of the material. It should not be used too early on in the life of a supervision group as it could deplete a vulnerable student's ego strength. As confidence grows so this form of reporting grows in popularity – 'memory training in action'.

FOCUSING ON AN INDIVIDUAL

This fruitful procedure can be useful if a student feels stuck about a particular patient, or if a drop-out is threatened, or indeed has occurred. It may be a vulnerable time and the student may need guiding through a review, or 'stock-take' as a learning process, e.g. recapitulation of the patient's background; account of involvement and evolvement in the group; what progress has been made; what needs special attention; any events that need focusing on. A patient's behaviour and participation in a particular group, or throughout several groups, may be explored in depth. Using this method, individual patients do not get neglected and problem areas can be highlighted.

KALEIDOSCOPIC APPROACH

A reasonably accurate script of a group is presented and students are asked to role-play, to settle into characters (whom they probably know quite well by now), then relay how they felt and experienced the group. The supervisor can participate too; the therapist is asked to sit outside the circle and observe. Any non-participant will be asked for comments and finally the therapist is asked to respond and report any new learning from this event. A different idea about a particular patient may evolve, but only an 'idea'. Reality needs to be checked with the real group.

This method has frequently proved to be energising and stimulates enthusiasm. It is an especially useful technique when supervising the large groups of around ten which are typical of the Institute of Group Analysis's block training abroad. Everyone can play a part in the ensuing discussion.

A variation on the idea is to stop the action at various points and ask the stand-in group members their perception of the process: 'What is going on?', 'What is happening now?', 'What do you feel?'

THEORETICAL ANALYSIS

The presenter focuses on a particular idea or concept such as transference/counter-transference, mirroring, resistance, etc., applied to the understanding of clinical material. When students are immersed in their theoretical training and want to understand its application to the real material of their groups, this method assists comprehension and evaluation of data.

BRAINSTORMING

A problem is brought and everyone offers spontaneous thoughts; one member jots these down. This helps the students to think and freely associate; it stops them becoming too intellectual. They have to think on their feet in their groups and this promotes agility and flexibility.

Vignette

A student's car broke down on her way to her group and she was delayed by one hour. Whilst the vehicle was being towed away, she fretted about what to say to the group when she arrived.

The supervisor stopped the action and asked the supervision group to offer spontaneous thoughts about how to deal with this situation. Ideas tumbled out: 'Tell them the truth'; 'Reality can impinge on the group'; 'It's not your fault, you should explain'; 'Why did you not check your car? Could it be your resistance to the group? Were you ambivalent about the group?'

The student continued her presentation. When she arrived in the group room, the group was in progress and nobody acknowledged her presence or late arrival. She felt invisible, a failure, the group did not need her. She ended the group at the usual time and left feeling vulnerable and tense.

This example of external events upsetting the equilibrium of a trainee clearly illustrates the need for the supervisor and group to offer support. In fact the supervision group empathised with her anxiety. 'You have the makings of an analyst,' said one of the more experienced members, 'because you had the courage to sit back, to wait and to do nothing.'

WRITTEN SUMMARY

In order to use the limited time available as constructively as possible, James Gustafson (Gustafson 1980) recommends using this method. A summary is given to the supervisor and the group in advance of the seminar. This provides optimum discussion time and is a valuable approach to adopt on occasions.

VISUAL AIDS TO PRESENTATION

Flip chart

This is preferable to a blackboard and colours can be used to advantage. A visual chart of seating arrangements in the groups can be illuminating if studied carefully over a period. Physical movement of the group members and/or the therapist may be indicative of something. For example, it became clear that a patient who usually tried to sit opposite the therapist to 'keep an eye' on him would sit next to him before and after a group break. (This is in a group where the therapist had a 'fixed' seat.)

Coding

Murray Cox's (Cox 1988) manual, 'Coding the therapeutic process', is a most useful conceptual tool and students use his display system occasionally.

Video

Skill is needed to use this. The group needs to be comfortable and the therapist has to cope with extra responsibilities if on video. It has strength as a teaching tool, although it can be tedious. It has been successfully used as a training facility in psychiatric clinics where a 'group-in-action' can be watched by all the trainee therapists with the trainer commenting simultaneously. It may be somewhat daunting and inhibiting to a 'beginner' therapist who is being viewed. The distinguished American group therapist Dr Irving Yalom, Professor of Psychiatry at Stanford University, California, has published a set of videotapes that offer typical group events, followed by his comments on his technique and understanding of the situation.[1] It is extremely helpful to see a 'master class'.

One-way mirror

This facility can demonstrate an experienced therapist at work. A follow-up discussion assists students to link the clinical material with theory.

CONCLUSION

Some of the more important tools available to the supervisor in the development of trainees have been highlighted. It is not appropriate to be didactic about the relative benefits or deficiencies of each approach. Good supervisors will want both to utilise their personal skills and experience, and also to experiment in developing individual portfolios of methods which work most effectively for them, and for their embryo group analysts.

NOTE

1 Enquiries to Irving Yalom, MD, Stanford University Medical Center, Stanford, California 94305, USA.

REFERENCES

Balint, E. (1993) in J. Mitchell and M. Parsons (eds) *Before I was I: Psychoanalysis and the Imagination*, London: Free Association Books.

Cox, M. (1988) *Emblems of Encounter: A Manual for Counsellors and Therapists*, London: Jessica Kingsley.

Gustafson, J.P. (1980) 'Group therapy supervision: critical problems of theory and technique', in L. Wolberg and M. Aronson (eds) *Group and Family Therapy*, New York: Jason Aronson.

Chapter 5

Difficulties and conflicts

Adele Mittwoch

Supervision is a lovesome thing – but is it always? Like a garden it needs toil and tender nurturing so that it can flourish. Unfortunately 'the course of true love never did run smooth' (Shakespeare, *A Midsummer Night's Dream* 1.i.134), and we have to suffer obstacles and setbacks. I will examine in this chapter some sources of difficulties and how to tackle them within the context of our creative endeavour. This context must be there. We cannot drop a stitch before we have learnt to knit, nor can we ring 'Gardeners' Question Time' before we know the basics of soils and fertilisers. Supervision does not begin until the trainee has demonstrated within his own therapy his flair for analytic process and his potential for conducting an analytic group.[1]

THE THIRD EYE WATCHES

All of us who have shared the supervisory experience would surely agree with Cohen *et al.* (1991: 53) that 'Supervision is an immensely stimulating and exciting aspect of our work as group analysts, whether as supervisor or supervisee'. We cannot but also agree with Sharpe (1991) that it takes courage to expose oneself to one's colleagues, whether one is a student or a group analyst. In other words it takes courage to expose oneself to criticism.

Yes, the trainee is keen to get going but he also feels anxious. More often than not he welcomes the watchful eye of the shepherd who keeps his flock out of danger, but the supervisor can also become for him the harsh superego, the driving test examiner who sits poised to write down every mistake, and who has power to fail the learner. I would go further than that, because exposure in front of one's contemporaries compounds the uneasy feeling. I often wonder whether the student's anxiety when starting the training group is more the fear of supervision than the fear of his patients.

I remember one student who had run a group successfully without supervision for a number of years, but went into a panic state before his first presentation of this group in the IGA. He reminded me of a patient who harboured a most painful memory of accomplishing the highest jump in his class at school, but who at the moment of landing broke wind. While the fart resounded through the gymnasium the teacher reassured the child with 'that can happen', but the shameful memory of the other children's barely suppressed grins persisted. This patient was on the road to recovery when he told of this unfortunate experience in the group. He no longer confined himself to the extremes of the omnipotence/impotence continuum and had a more realistic attitude to himself. Likewise the panic-ridden student regained his composure, and in general shame in the supervision seminar tends to subside as trainees come to realise that there is no perfect group or perfect conductor, and that every group has something to offer. This insight may take a long time to acquire, and I will return to this topic in the next section. Meanwhile I must deal with some practical issues.

The student conducting his training group sits there worrying about remembering it all. In those circumstances does he pay the right kind of attention to his group? Is he spontaneous in his interventions? There is no simple way of overcoming these difficulties. I do not think that recording equipment is the answer. In fact I dislike too full and detailed a report. It is like being unable to see the wood for the trees. I prefer a report of no more than half an hour even though it is selective, as long as the student does not withhold his own interventions.

Students afraid of 'teacher power' sometimes ask or demand to see the supervisor's report to the Training Committee, or even to be involved in the writing of the report. I do not generally comply with such demands; I am just not 'with it'. I feel that we need to use the time to hear about the groups and deal with real difficulties, rather than to assuage paranoia. This would not succeed anyway; I am reminded of a group member who demanded to see his file but was told by the others that he could not see his therapist's thoughts. I do sometimes, when the spirit moves me, let the students see what I have written.

THE BEGINNER'S PROBLEM: DO I HAVE SOMETHING TO OFFER?

A student presented the first session of his training group. The patients were depressed, whingeing, complaining, aggressive and they scapegoated. The apparent absence of any anxiety was striking, as was the absence of any expression of hope grounded in the idea that this might be the start of a new curative venture. Ensuing reports contained scant evidence of any positive shift but rather contained the added ingredients of expressions of frustration and threats of leaving the group. I admired my supervisee's ability to carry on with such an unrewarding group, I almost envied him, but at the same time I urged him to try to bring about some relief by providing a nurturing climate and fostering trust. The trainee, it emerged, was not appreciative of help for himself in his twice-weekly therapy group, compared with the help that he had received in the past, when he underwent psychoanalysis five times a week.

Years later another student kept losing patients out of his training group mostly for reasons beyond his control. Again this situation mirrored that in his twice-weekly group in which he did not feel secure. The oppressive atmosphere in both training groups lifted when the trainees became convinced of the benefit they were deriving from their therapy groups and when they stopped measuring loving care in terms of the amount of time spent. A story of mine that has appeared elsewhere (Mittwoch 1991: 88) is helpful in making students appreciate the value of treatment even when sessions are widely spaced. I reproduce the story here:

> George was a member of a therapeutic social club. One day I commented on how well he looked. 'Yes, I feel well', he said, 'and I am making very good progress in my analysis.' What he meant by analysis was a ten minute appointment every six weeks with a psychiatrist! Dr X not only kept an eye on George's medication and gave a pep talk, he also tended to supply at least one interpretation.

The point of this story is that anything can be 'enough' provided the patient gives his heart to it and keeps up the momentum. I also tell students about Robin Skynner's dictum (I am not sure whether he ever committed it to print): he was more and more convinced that there is no such thing as a deprived patient. What causes the feeling of deprivation is the mother's feeling of guilt, usually quite unfounded, of not providing enough. This dictum was of particular relevance to a third supervisee whose training group went very well, but who was nevertheless plagued with the notion that his patients would derive a lot more benefit if their group conductor wore the mantle of long experience, such as the mantle worn by his therapist and also by his supervisor. This trainee perked up further, as did his fellow supervisees, when I suggested that trainees approach their work with wonder, excitement and the greatest conscientiousness, while their

elders who embody received wisdom may have to fight off a tendency
to drop off to sleep in the middle of sessions. The penny dropped, I heard
the click and saw four gleeful faces.

ANOTHER BEGINNER'S PROBLEM: I HAVE COMMITTED THE ULTIMATE SIN

I am indebted to Graeme Farquharson for the following example which
derives from supervision of groups within a residential setting: A young
member of staff reported a dream of the previous night which was
highly erotic and specific to a member of his group. The dreamer, who
was deeply ashamed, 'confessed' to it in the seminar only because he
was so troubled, but expected to be dismissed. He was astonished when
the dream and his feelings about it were taken up at a level to be
understood, rather than be acted against. In fact the incident provided
valuable learning for him and others. They worked within a population
rife with sexual abuse, but the young staff often denied their vulnerability and sexuality.

By way of digression I will here mention another difficulty which is
a bit like the previous vignette in reverse: occasionally it is necessary to
draw a student's attention to his attire or demeanour when these are
rather seductive. However delicately I try to approach the matter it is
likely to cause some anger and distress. It is really helpful on such
occasions to have the opinion of other seminar members, so that con-
sensus can be reached.

THE GROUP-ANALYTIC FRATERNITY[2]

Competition is a *sine qua non* within any group of siblings, and naturally
our students compete with one another within the seminar group. This is
all right within reasonable limits as it leads to effort and good work.
Competitiveness between students can, however, become destructive
and intimidating, especially when it is not recognised. When brought
into the open any crisis situation of this nature is usually quickly
resolved. My own nursery training took place in a supervision seminar
run by Pat de Maré before the IGA Qualifying Course had been established. This seminar not only was a lovesome thing, but it also contra-
vened the Shakespearean rule quoted above in as much as the course of
true love always did seem to run smooth. I well remember a fellow
student calling out, 'I like this supervision seminar. Here I can present
my group without feeling that it is bottom.' In a formal training I would

not expect such a Utopian state of affairs, but the experience helped me
to be alert to danger signals.

What about competition amongst teaching staff? As a supervisor I
refuse to compete with theory teachers. I expect my students to be
familiar with theoretical concepts that we use to understand the clinical
material. If students demand more theory from me I refer them to their
teaching seminar or possibly provide a reference to the literature. Above
all, as the supervisor, I refuse to compete with the student's therapist. I
firmly stick to running a didactic seminar, and I enjoin any students with
difficulties that are rooted in their unconscious to take these difficulties
to their therapy group. This may not always be necessary in the case of
certain advanced students. I remember one of them who reported that he
had to absent himself quite unexpectedly in the middle of a group
session because of an urgent call of nature. He was able to analyse his
own counter-transference and got in touch with hitherto repressed anger.
We learnt that the group had started post-session meetings in the pub
with destructive consequences. In the light of this explanation the
student's self-analysis made sense and no further action was necessary.

Here is an example of fruitful co-operation between supervisor and
therapist:

> We became aware that a student halfway through his final year
> had a rapid turnover of patients in his training group. People just
> stayed away, letters hardly ever went out, and after a month or two
> these patients were written off without ado. The student, a psy-
> chiatric registrar, replaced these drop-outs with other patients
> from the waiting list and reported sessions as though nothing was
> amiss. When we commented on what seemed to us a lackadaisical
> way of going about things, the student became defensive and
> argumentative. He felt that patients should not be 'forced to stay'.
> Finally he burst into tears, saying that he knew that he was 'the
> worst student on the course'. It occurred to us that he wanted to
> leave his own therapy group at the end of the year and that he was
> anxious lest he was considered not ready. We encouraged him to
> bring these anxieties to the therapy group; in this case I had to
> approach the therapist myself, who handled the matter sensitively.
> After a few weeks the student's clinical work and self-evaluation
> had improved.

In the last example, a trainee therapist projected his own unconscious
wishes on to his patients. Another difficulty is that of the person who has
seemingly overcome a problem, only to displace it on to someone else.

I have previously described at length the seemingly magic cure of a person whom I observed in a non-clinical setting (Mittwoch 1987: 337). In brief:

> A former colleague of mine, given to severe hypochondriasis, had been unreliable in his attendances for many years. When his boss lost his temper this man did a turn-around and he never had occasion to stay away from work again. The cure however was not radical because he got married and started to fuss about his wife's health.

The following example derives from supervision:

> The student's training group had a history of many crises, both within sessions and outside them, when the student would be contacted by the hospital to provide emergency treatment. Now this student's own behaviour in the past had been full of high drama, although he was now much more composed. I wondered whether he had some personal investment in his patients' catastrophic situation. When I gently voiced this he sharply attacked me for 'always criticising' him, and tears followed. At the same time he volunteered the information that he had already begun to tackle this difficulty in his therapy. We had a useful discussion in which we noted his patients' behaviour reflecting that of his former self. Further work took place in the student's therapy group, and his patients in tandem calmed down and became less demanding.

Other supervisors work differently, by analysing the members' unconscious hang-ups. In some supervisory situations this is appropriate, i.e. where the students are not in analysis. Within the IGA, however, secondary therapeutic groups could lead to splitting, which is not to my liking, although I have not heard of detrimental happenings from my colleagues. On the contrary, the multiple therapy arrangement may suit some training group analysts. I know of one occasion where a therapist refused to give attention to a trainee analysand who had an obvious difficulty *vis-à-vis* a patient of his who reminded him of his younger brother. The therapist maintained that his group was not concerned with training and he referred the matter back to supervision. The supervisor had difficulty fighting it out with his therapist colleague and some bad feeling remained.

Most of our students receive supervision at their places of work as well as in the IGA. Hospital consultants usually confine their supervisory function to the progress of each of their patients, and they are not interested in the group dynamics, which is the proper concern of the IGA seminar. Such dual supervision is not rivalrous and the two learning situations complement one another. This, however, is not universal. The 'other supervision seminar' can at times stand for the 'other woman' or, at a deeper level, for the 'other parent'. Students can become confused when conflicting advice is offered, they can occasionally play up one 'parent' against the other. Oh Oedipus! The best thing to do is to confront the other party.

Another difficulty between colleagues is more in the mind than actual, the difficulty resulting from what I am tempted to call 'the sins of the fathers'. Certain students in their first term are overkeen to get their groups off the ground and rush through the preliminary interviews. During this term all IGA first-year students are together in one large seminar. Important issues may not be attended to at the interview stage and these omissions may not come to light until difficulties arise at a much later stage in training. Patients may have joined a group without knowing in advance that the group will be time-limited, and/or they may not have entered into a contract of commitment for a sufficiently long period of time. In such circumstances it is easy to blame the 'fathers', comprising the first-term supervisor and everyone responsible for the structure of the course, which puts too great a demand on the first-term supervisor. Now that the course has been lengthened perhaps we will be spared this kind of difficulty in the future.

THE FORMATIVE YEARS

Students enter the course with firmly established professional identities. They feel secure in their work as doctors, nurses, social workers, psychologists, teachers, clergymen, etc. The task in training is to acquire and integrate the group-analytic attitude which, in the words of Foulkes, 'ought to become so much part of the person that he does not have to think how to apply it . . .' (see Mittwoch 1980). On the whole the newly acquired facet of identity sits easily on the composite structure. Occasionally there is conflict.

Possibly the greatest difficulties have arisen in the training of ministers of religion who might have too great an inclination towards self-sacrifice. Hard and fast rules regarding identity do not exist; we do not set out to train clones. I am identified as an analyst irrespective of whether I work with individuals or groups. I would find family therapy with its more directive technique incompatible, and yet others engage effectively in both kinds of work. I am not sure that transactional analysis or Gestalt work can easily be interspersed with group-analytic work.

Kennard *et al.* (1990) have been much concerned with the distinguishing identity of the group analyst. I think we would all agree that group analysis, like psychoanalysis, is not an exact science, and to me the cornerstone in analytic work is avoidance of either–or thinking (Schafer 1983). I therefore have an aversion to therapists asking questions and many a rub in supervision can arise out of that.

The group analyst at the end of training may undergo an identity crisis, as described by King (1983). The supervisor does well to bear this in mind right through the training in order to dislodge his students from cloud-cuckoo land.

At the end of this chapter I return to my gardening analogy. Certain plants may not be thriving for a time because of their individual characteristics. They may need special attention or treatment or may have to be moved to another place in the garden. The reader may ask whether in extreme cases a plant may have to be moved altogether to another more suitable garden. This, figuratively, occasionally happens in the training of individual therapists when a supervisor's theoretical orientation is seriously at odds with that of the student. As far as I know this has never been necessary in the IGA. Each supervisor has his own style, but we also form a uniform breed whose members encourage and support one another. Such a substratum is fertile ground for our trainees.

NOTES

1   In this chapter the masculine pronoun also encompasses the feminine. This style of writing serves the interest of confidentiality and avoids clumsy expressions such as 'he or she'.
2   This heading may not be politically correct but, as with my pronouns, sexism is not implied. I use the word 'fraternity' in the sense of one of the OCD definitions of 'a group or company with common interest, or of the same professional class'.

REFERENCES

Cohen, V., McGrath, P. and Sharpe, J. (1991) 'The supervisory seminar', in Part 1 of 'Countertransference and therapist change: an aspect of supervision', *Group Analysis* 24(1): 53–62.

Kennard, D., Roberts, J. and Winter, D. (1990) 'What do group analysts say in their groups? Some results from the IGA/GAS questionnaire', *Group Analysis* 23(2): 173–183.

King, P. (1983) 'Identity crises: splits or compromises – adaptive or maladaptive', in E.D. Joseph and D. Widlöcher (eds) *The Identity of the Psychoanalyst*, New York: International Universities Press.

Mittwoch, A. (1980) 'The professional identity and future of the group analyst (meeting report)', *Group Analysis* 13(3): 212–214.

Mittwoch, A. (1987) 'Getting better, staying well', *Group Analysis* 20(4): 335–342.

Mittwoch, A. (1991) 'The once-weekly groups', in J. Roberts and M. Pines (eds) *The Practice of Group Analysis*, London: Routledge.

Schafer, R. (1983) *The Analytic Attitude*, London: Hogarth Press and Institute of Psycho-Analysis.

Sharpe, M. (1991) 'Discussion on paper by Cohen *et al.*', *Group Analysis* 24(1): 63.

Chapter 6

Monitoring the supervisee

Vivienne Cohen

The clinical and theoretical component of the Qualifying Course of the Institute of Group Analysis spans three academic years, during which time students are required to conduct two weekly groups under supervision at the Institute. The first training group is set up in the second term and is a mixed adult outpatient stranger group of psychoneurotic patients which continues throughout the training period and longer if so required by the Training Committee; there is no obligation to terminate this group at the end of the training period. The second, recently introduced, is set up at the end of the second year to commence at the beginning of the final year and is an approved time-limited patient group which terminates at the end of the course and which reflects the many different interests and work experiences of the students, for example inpatient groups, children's groups, groups for elderly patients, couples' groups, groups of women sexually abused in childhood and other homogeneous or single-sex groups.

This chapter is concerned with supervision of the first training group. Supervision takes place once weekly in seminar groups of four students, usually from different-year cohorts. There is continuous assessment and feedback in the seminar throughout the training but every second term (that is, in the first, third, fifth, seventh and ninth terms) supervisors submit a formal report to the Training Committee on the progress of the students in their supervision group; a report is presented termly if there is concern about a student's progress.

There is considerable diversity in supervisors' styles of appraisal and feedback, and in the extent to which mutual feedback takes place (Sharpe and Blackwell 1987). There is less variation in the content of reports to the Training Committee: reference would be made to aspects such as presentation, style of conducting, capacity to contain the group and establish trust, to maintain boundaries, to work analytically with the group, to handle problem situations and to work using counter-transference. Any special difficulties would be described and comment offered on the student's participation in the seminar. The content of such reports is well illustrated by the following extracts (all names used are pseudonyms).

'Julian's group continues to develop effectively. Members have been much preoccupied lately with guilt and shame, and Julian has facilitated increasingly open expression of feelings and exploration. The whole group has been going through an angry phase which he has handled well.

I had to miss three supervision seminars at the beginning of term and A (another supervisor) generously took care of the sessions in my absence. Julian had been very anxious about this arrangement, anticipating that A would be a severe taskmaster but in the event found it a valuable and facilitating experience. Julian's severity with himself, of course, played a part in this painful anticipation, but he is certainly now more kindly to himself and more permissive to the group, and the old puritanical streak is less evident.

Recently a first-year student in the seminar was describing the considerable anger expressed by members of his training group. Julian, with great honesty and integrity, contrasted this with his own training group which had taken until the third or fourth term to express anything like as much anger. He acknowledged not only his difficulties with anger, with which we were already familiar, but his problems of trusting, this difficulty in trusting thus being reflected in the group's difficulty in trusting him.

He is the quietest member of the supervision seminar and makes few interventions; those that he does make are always of interest, although occasionally more pertinent to his work than to the presenter's.

Although lacking sparkle, he is a reliable, steadfast, stolid and solid conductor, intelligent and thoughtful and responsive to counter-transference exploration. I think he would benefit from learning how to "play" a little more, but this may yet develop.'

The following series of reports provides a profile of a student's progress and personal development. This student worked very hard and courageously in the face of very many disadvantages. He had been seconded from abroad, separated from his wife and family, on an inadequate stipend granted for the bare minimum training period. He lived in penury, his previous training in psychotherapy was considerably more limited than his sponsoring institution had led us to believe, and at the beginning his spoken English was imperfect.

Term 2

'Apart from the occasions when he has presented, Eduardo has been extremely quiet in the seminar; I do not think this is to do with his linguistic difficulties but is the way in which he deals with his anxiety and great sense of inadequacy. His anxiety also tends to make him excessively silent in his training group.

He often looks quite lost and anxious, like a deprived child, and tries to get a little extra time at the beginning or end of a supervision session. . . . I sometimes get the impression that he really is literally cold and hungry, both physically and emotionally. I am sure he finds the lengthy separation from his family and his highly impoverished existence in an alien environment extremely difficult. His obsessional traits are particularly evident when we discuss the handling of patients who have missed a session – in such situations he is impelled to write down every word and I often have to tell him to stop writing and to listen.

Despite this his group seems to be developing well and Eduardo has been able to present cogently and intelligently and to share with the seminar group his counter-transference difficulties. I think he will shape out well despite all the problems with which he has to contend.'

Term 3

'Eduardo seems to be able to enjoy his group more but is still extremely anxious at times, especially when he is afraid of losing control. His need to write down everything that is said in a seminar has lessened slightly and he does allow himself more contact with his own inner anxieties. However, he still wants to be taught the "right way" to do things and has difficulty in being spontaneous.

At a recent seminar we explored his counter-transference difficulties with a patient who, having indicated that there were many things she could not communicate to the group, disclosed some of her inner chaos through slightly bizarre behaviour. Eduardo was finding the situation very difficult to handle and seemed to feel completely at a loss with her; he had, in fact, appeared rather frightened of what this patient might do from her very first session. On this occasion I suggested that it may be that she stood for the parts of himself that clearly wanted to go out of control and to behave in an outlandish, crazy, demanding and aggressive manner. He agreed with a rather sheepish grin and looked quite relieved to have this brought out in the open.

Despite all the difficulties that he is struggling with, he does not seem to be totally blocked and, as always, much will depend on his progress in therapy.'

Term 5

'I am concerned about Eduardo's progress, because it is still very slow and his quite inadequate grant is due to come to an end in nine months. In the seminar group he has needed a great deal of attention, but it is the persistence of his almost obsessional need to record, rather than to listen to what is said, which has provoked irritation, rather than his neediness which has been well understood and tolerated. He is a concerned therapist, a diligent student and struggles hard despite many practical difficulties.

Although he has always been outwardly courteous and considerate, I have throughout been aware of an internal struggle with compliance/defiance and this recently came to a head as a result of a confrontation in a seminar between Eduardo and myself about his compulsive writing. Eduardo was distressed by the confrontation and afterwards I spent half an hour with him individually; on this occasion he seemed more in contact with these two parts of himself, rather than simply knowing of their existence, and I think the result has been quite a considerable shift.'

Following this, Eduardo was able to negotiate a further term's leave of absence and an extension at a reduced level of his inadequate grant.

Term 7

'Over the past six months he has relaxed considerably from his rigid and almost obsessional previous style. He seems to have been able to make some headway towards a resolution of his internal struggle between compliance/defiance; this development was considerably facilitated by the confrontation between Eduardo and myself in the seminar last spring. He subsequently acknowledged that this incident helped towards a substantial working on the conflict between the two aspects of himself in his own therapy group.

His decision to negotiate a further term on the Qualifying Course and my thus being able to offer him another patient to replace members who had left, played a further part in allowing him to develop, as some of the sense of urgency, panic and failure was reduced.

Latterly, as he has been able to absorb more from the seminar, his neediness has waned and is no longer a feature. He no longer asks to be taught the "right way" to do things and, occasionally, he is even able to toy with a concept, and thus make it his own, before using it. . . . I do not think he will become a natural and intuitively informed therapist, but I am hopeful that by the end of his additional term of training he will be competent enough to acquit himself well when he returns to his university hospital.'

Students' difficulties are discussed very fully in the Training Committee and much care and considerable effort is put into helping each develop his or her full potential. An 'early warning system' ensures that when there is concern about a student's progress reports are received and considered every term; training group analysts are invited at their discretion to the meetings and where appropriate are sent copies of the reports.

A student's progress as a therapist is, of course, intimately intertwined with the personal development that centres on his or her own psychotherapy, and sometimes a training group's progress may almost come to standstill awaiting change in the conductor. At other times students' experiences with the groups they are conducting, or in supervision, may stimulate personal growth (Cohen *et al.* 1991). The following examples illustrate these two situations.

1 Simon

About two terms after beginning his training group at Bart's, Simon obtained a post at a considerable distance from London. Although he continued with the full Qualifying Course training programme – personal group analysis, academic seminars, training group and supervision – he was no longer able to attend the supervision seminar at Bart's. After he had been conducting his group for a year I wrote:

'I am very unhappy about Simon's therapeutic work . . . his biggest problem has been that of tending to distance himself from the patients. This has been especially powerful when they have expressed ambivalence about continuing and at such times he would almost withdraw from contact as if he wanted to leave them before they left him. Being handicapped by such a difficulty in reaching out to patients, he has had a very high drop-out throughout. This has improved latterly, but has not ceased, and I am concerned about his work; no present or previous Qualifying Course student at Bart's has had as heavy a drop-out. I have told him that I cannot offer him more new patients until he has learnt to hold the ones he has and that this was something he would have to continue to deal with in his personal therapy.

He has about a year longer with this group and it is crucially important that he achieves a change very soon. I think it would be helpful to discuss his progress with his Institute supervisor and perhaps his group analyst; I hope that they will be able to be present at the Training Committee meeting.'

The training group analyst was unable to be present at the Training Committee meeting, but sent the following comments: 'This is the only candidate about whom I have reservations.' Reference is then made to the progress he had made, and continues:

'He is much more able to relate to others in the group, but still cuts off and detaches himself when under pressure that might stimulate negative feelings in him, although, as the group has pointed out, he is able to show and accept positive feelings much more easily. He tends to function in terms of an idealised self related to an idealised, but very strange, father . . .'

At the Training Committee meeting his Institute supervisor commented that she never really knew what was happening in his group and the Committee gave considerable thought to these reports, even questioning whether Simon should be allowed to remain in training. After careful consideration, following the meeting I wrote to the training group analyst.

'. . . his work with the group has been far from satisfactory throughout, although it has improved latterly. His biggest problem, as I see it, is his very high rate of drop-out. He and I have managed to look at the circumstances surrounding the

departure of the last two or three patients and this has confirmed and made him aware of what was fairly evident all
along, that is, that he is unable to reach out in any way to people
in distress when he is uncertain how they will respond.
Coupled with this, he has always had a major difficulty in his
tendency to distance himself from the patients. This is especially powerful when they express ambivalence . . .'

After receiving these adverse reports the training group analyst at
a suitable moment in the group (when several members, including
Simon, were talking about work) took the unusual step of confronting Simon with, 'I think you should really speak to your
supervisors as it seems to me that you are not picking up the same
message that I have been receiving'. Simon became really furious,
but after that worked very much harder and made much more
progress, progress which continued steadily until six months later
I was able to write:

'I am very happy to report that Simon has changed and is at last
able to make real contact with his patients with the result that
the group is working well, has become cohesive and much
more active. At the same time he has been able to feel closer
and be truly kinder to the patients; he has also learnt to be a lot
firmer and this combination has led to a great increase in the
sense of security that the patients experience. Interestingly
enough, a very difficult, hostile man who had been a problem
patient in a previous therapeutic situation, and who had done
exceptionally well in this group in the hands of the rather
remote and "cut off" Simon, withdrew when Simon became
more involved. As well as being responsive to the change, the
group has actually commented on it.

In supervision he has been very honest about his counter-
transference difficulties and has ceased to behave defensively.
His presentations are clearer and more cogent than in the past,
he comes across as a more genuine person and no longer causes
me to feel concerned.'

My final report three months later:

'I am delighted with Simon's continued progress. He is working effectively, is able to be both facilitating and firm and no
longer has to distance himself from the patients. He is handling
the approaching ending of the group responsibly and sensibly

and is freely in touch with his own feelings. Simon's presentations are now interesting, lively and pertinent and include an engaging honesty about mistakes he has made in the present and in the past . . .'

2 Daniel

Daniel's development was given a spurt by an event in supervision two months before the end of his training and the termination of his training group and his own group analysis. It was also his penultimate day at work before moving and Alex, the leader of the team with which he had worked for many years, had asked him to lunch. He felt unable to accept because it clashed with the supervision seminar and Alex drove him to the station instead. On the train he opened his briefcase, took out the group notes and jotted down a few ideas. He thought about the termination of the group and felt guilty that this had come about because he needed to move and take up new work and recognised that these feelings had been reflected in the content of the session – that what was taking place in him was taking place in the patients.

At supervision it was Daniel's turn to present and he opened his briefcase. His face became ashen and he looked transfixed. His notes were gone. He sat in horrified silence and afterwards recorded his feelings:

'In a flash I saw the notes on the seat beside me in the train. Feelings of loneliness, despair, impotence, betrayal, rage, flooded me together with somatic symptoms, coldness, thirst, sweating, stomach pains, aching joints and dizziness. Ideas raced into my mind as excusing explanations, for I felt like a criminal which stirred in me several half-glimpsed memories. I was very confused and felt completely gripped by forces beyond my control. Frozen, I started to cry deeply inside. Like the baby who has given up crying outside because no one is there.

I began without the notes to speak about the group, about its ending and my concern but it was not possible for me to focus upon or remember the group for I felt myself in pieces. Dislocated, I tried to make sense of the lost notes while offering the group and myself for supervision.'

I asked him if he would like to look at the loss of the notes. He said he would but sat unable to speak. I asked was it to do with not wanting to be here today, wanting to go out to lunch instead. He licked his dry lips. 'Is it about not wanting to be here, about doing what you think you ought to do, not what you want to do?' Daniel struggled to reply: 'Yes, it was about not wanting to come to supervision, and wanting to be in my office for the lunch and the celebration with Alex. It's also about endings; Alex cannot deal with endings and so I feel defeated thinking of trying to say goodbye to him. It is also about ending supervision, and missing you, and saying goodbye to you, and to all the training.' I said, 'That makes a lot of sense. I think there is also something more, something you are not in contact with that suddenly overwhelms you and takes all the life out of you. Perhaps there was a significant moment in your life when there were similar feelings about not wanting to be somewhere . . . about putting yourself under obligation.'

Daniel, moist-eyed, told us of his experience during the war at the age of four (an event already much worked on therapeutically) when he and his mother were evacuated to a very poor farmhouse. His mother left him with the family and returned to London. Daniel shared his sense of abandonment with the supervision group, linking his forlorn anticipation of the ending of training to his feelings as an evacuee. He also shared with us the despairing sense of abandonment that he experienced when desperately ill with tuberculosis at the age of ten. He had been told also of his premature birth early in the war, in a hospital where all available space was filled with the wounded from Dunkirk and a fragile baby was a burden, and he was able now to make some sense of this. He recalled the overwhelming feeling of emptiness when his mother repeatedly told him how much suffering he had caused and he remembered experiencing the same physical symptoms as today.

Daniel later recorded: 'The echoes of these significant moments resonated deeply within me and in working at the incidents in supervision, taking it to my therapy group and tenaciously staying with the maelstrom of thoughts and feelings that engulfed me I gradually became more settled and experienced myself as being intensely familiar with my own history. It was as if separated parts of my life had come together more completely than I had ever known.'

His training group, too, worked tenaciously and intensely towards termination and spoke of despair and abandonment and of falling apart.

Supervisors' progress reports frequently mirror comments from the training group analyst, sometimes unknowingly even using the same words. For example, in the case of Julian described at the beginning of this chapter, the training group analyst had also used the phrase 'sometimes seeming almost puritanical' and, on the same occasion as the supervisor's report quoted above, noted that 'he needs occasionally to be reminded to relate himself to what he is saying to another', and also 'he drives himself hard . . . but is allowing himself to be gentler with others (and himself)'.

Another kind of mirroring that occurs in supervision is where the student's reporting of his or her training group more accurately mirrors the student's own inner life than that of the group, as in the following example, and of course a student's personal difficulties may distort his presentation of the training group, or even be projected on to the training group, especially if the student is in a 'stuck' phase.

Kenneth's group had gone through a rather intense phase, followed by a run of absenteeism and a good deal of lateness, which then settled down. The supervisor reported:

'Throughout all this, the group most of the time seemed to work responsively, shared a good deal of warmth and mutual concern, and was able to absorb a newcomer. Kenneth, however, appeared increasingly worried about the group and reached a point where he seemed to have a struggle recalling the details of the sessions, and his presentation became uncharacteristically confusing. He said of one particular session that the group seemed to be pulling away, distancing, and I commented that in the seminar itself it was he who had exuded a sense of distance and could he be projecting some of his own feelings on to the group? He then realised that the group had actually been dealing with closeness, the members had become closer to each other and perhaps also to him and the closeness presented a problem for him. This incident seemed to create a real breakthrough for him, and both in the seminar and in his conducting style he has become stronger and there is a more positive sense of his presence. There was another wobbly patch a couple of months later, when Kenneth felt that the group was chaotic and disintegrating, which it was not, but what he was feeling about the group accurately represented his own feelings at the time . . .'

The salient point that emerges is that the task of evaluating and monitoring supervisees essentially involves the principles of group analysis. Supervisors combine limited therapeutic activity with their supervisory role, functioning more as conductors than as teachers, and although the supervision seminar is not a therapeutic group it is a setting in which much therapy takes place. Supervision and therapy are the twin pedestals of a student's development and a student's progress as a therapist is crucially dependent on his or her own progress in therapy – the two are inextricably entangled.

REFERENCES

Cohen, V., McGrath, P. and Sharpe, J. (1991) 'Countertransference and therapist change: an aspect of supervision', *Group Analysis* 24(1): 53–63.

Sharpe, M. and Blackwell, D. (1987) 'Creative supervision through student involvement', *Group Analysis* 20(3): 195–208.

Chapter 7

Supervision in the National Health Service

Robin Sproul-Bolton
Morris Nitsun
Jane Knowles

Part I Group supervision in an acute psychiatric unit

Robin Sproul-Bolton

The setting is relatively comfortable. It is an office set in a ground floor extension of a large detached square building in the grounds of a district general hospital. There is a circle of chairs and the door is open. Shortly after 3 p.m., six people walk in, some carrying mugs of tea. They sit down and shut the door. There is a brief hubbub of conversation before attention is focused on the task in hand. The familiar routine of group supervision has begun.

I am a full-time NHS group analyst working in what was once one of the charismatic and unique therapeutic communities that flourished briefly in the NHS during the 1970s. Its creation as an acute psychiatric unit within a district general hospital was challenging. Much of its treatment philosophy was based on the work of Maxwell Jones, Tom Main, S.H. Foulkes and others who pioneered the approach during and after the Second World War. The bulk of therapy revolved around a network of interlocking groups of which the daily 'large group' or community meeting formed the hub. Thus, ideas, emotions, and issues emerging from this forum, seeded the fertile ground of the small groups that followed after.

Naturally, this approach was stressful and demanded much teamwork and interdisciplinary co-operation. From the outset the concept of supervision was written into the daily programme as an essential ingredient in the process. A full-time group analyst was employed in recognition of the skills and complexities that good group work demanded.

The unit's role as a therapeutic community persisted through the 1970s but then began to decline in the 1980s, to be replaced by a more orthodox model based on current district general hospital acute psychiatric principles. Because of the unit's enduring tradition in group work, the post of group analyst survived, in spite of the changes that altered the unit's philosophy so fundamentally.

I see my role as helping to preserve this tradition. The role of group supervisor is therefore an important one. I am required to oversee and ensure that the broad range of therapeutic groups comprising this network of care survive and remain in good health. Newly appointed staff often comment on the time and effort that the unit considers appropriate to devote to supervision, perhaps because this is novel and unfamiliar to them.

THE 'NUTS AND BOLTS' OF SUPERVISION

Generally, I adopt a group approach to supervision. Not only is this cost-effective in terms of time, but it also offers unique advantages over seeing people individually. For example, a group can offer peer support. This is especially helpful for new or inexperienced staff who may view the whole process of supervision, with its connotations of criticism and possible humiliation, as fearful. Equally, there is the probability that information shared about other groups will enable staff to learn by example. Thus, there will be many gains from receiving reflections, feedback and sharing inputs not only from the supervisor but also from all members of the group.

Another advantage is that there will be less chance of the setting being unduly dominated by the supervisor. In individual supervision, dependency issues between supervisor and supervisee can prevent an objective view prevailing and result in unnecessary collusions occurring. In a group setting other members can challenge this, provided the group is functioning at a safe enough level. Groups of supervisees can offer a wide range of experiences, age ranges and points of view. This can provide a rich pool of knowledge that can help the supervisor arrive at a better understanding of the situation under review. It can also help younger, less experienced staff, who may be facing novel situations, feel less threatened and out of their depth. Typical are situations where patients or clients become disturbed in therapy and confront the relatively inexperienced therapist with abuse and/or aggressive behaviour.

Another important advantage of group supervision is that from a psychodynamic point of view, the supervision group can become a mirror, reflecting the situation under review. Thus, if the supervisor notices some unusual responses from the group, such as sleepiness or boredom, this may be a counter-transference response illuminating very graphically what the group is trying to understand intellectually. Often it is very valuable to ask the group what they are feeling in response to what is being presented, and using these responses as therapeutic pointers. It is also very valuable sometimes to use the supervisees as a cast of actors to role-play situations that are creating difficulties for the group. This will often reflect the dynamics of the situation more effectively than extensive debate.

There are of course disadvantages to supervising in a group. For example, not all members will be able to discuss their own case or group in the limited time available. Also, the group itself will develop its own dynamics that may cloud the dynamics of the group in question. If this is not monitored carefully, the process of supervision can be seriously undermined. This is especially so if transferences develop in the supervision group that block its objective vision. And so it is essential that the group supervisor ensures that group dynamics are addressed and if necessary discussed in the group so that a greater understanding can occur, but in such a way that it does not detract from the work of supervision.

While supervising, I take note of many aspects of what is going on. I am interested in the content of the group in question. I need to understand what has happened and how it has happened. I also need to know how this session relates to previous sessions in the history of the group.

I am interested in how the therapist understands this too. The nature of his or her interventions are very important, as are the tactics and strategies employed that arise out of these interventions. The language employed by the therapist is of special interest in that I want to know whether he or she is developing a style that facilitates free-floating discussion, as well as encouraging the expression of metaphor and imagery in the group. This will lead me to pay careful attention to what was expressed consciously or unconsciously in the group and to what extent the therapist was tuned in to these. I want to help the therapist to develop a way of lateral thinking that avoids arriving at premature, rigid ideas about what is going on in the session. Part of that process is a need to help the therapists to be aware of their own counter-transference, or at least that which is carried over into the supervision session from the group. This can comprise a number of forms. It could arise out of issues that belong to the therapist's own unresolved resistances. Or it could be the result of transference projections from members of the group that the therapist has taken in, either somatically or psychically.

While I am listening to a supervisee, I am also watching the other supervisees in order to see if, in any way, the group is mirroring unconsciously what is unfolding in the narrative. As I explained earlier, much can be learned from this process. Equally important is my own reaction to what is going on. I monitor my own counter-transference responses just as carefully as I observe the group. So often this is significant. The other day, I became bored in a supervision session. Normally this group is lively and holds my interest, but on this occasion people seemed distracted. Interaction between members of the group had died away. I caught myself wishing that the session would end. Now thoroughly aware of the situation, I asked members of the group what they were feeling at that moment. There was a pause and then the group began cautiously to admit to feelings of disconnection. Further exploration of this revealed the fact that the group under discussion had failed to acknowledge the anniversary of the leaving of a cherished therapist. In fact, the group had never properly mourned this loss. The present therapist was then able to disclose feelings of considerable hostility towards the other therapist, hitherto hidden.

Other issues of interest are of a pragmatic nature relating to the role of the therapist as dynamic administrator. I am concerned that proper boundaries are maintained and that the setting is adequate. I try to impress on the supervisees the need to safeguard the setting at all cost. Often this is difficult in the NHS because space is at a premium and staff are used to encroachments and invasions of their working areas. I try to encourage them to take a much less tolerant stance on these matters. I teach staff the need to observe other important boundaries such as the need to start and stop at the appointed hour. This often leads to discussions about rules. New therapists are often overpreoccupied with setting rules in order to feel more secure and to cover unpleasant future events in advance, such as: lateness (no one can come in after the first ten minutes), language (swearing will not be tolerated), prejudice (sexist comments will not be tolerated), etc. It is important, however, that essential rules are considered and implemented (physical violence will not be tolerated).

As regards my own style as a supervisor, I try to apply the principles that underpin my work as a therapist, in terms of the listening skill required, as a prerequisite to being a good supervisor. To this must be added the third ear of the psychotherapist.

AREAS COVERED BY SUPERVISION

The groups that I supervise can be sub-divided into:

- The large group;
- Focused groups;
- Community support groups;
- Outpatient groups.

The large group is of special interest. This is a direct legacy of the old therapeutic community. Miraculously it has survived all the changes and is, therefore, a very mature twenty-year-old group. It takes place daily and is open to anyone, both staff and patients. My role here is both as therapist and supervisor. As in the therapeutic community, a half hour is set aside after the group for feedback. It is during that time that I attempt to help the staff absorb the impact of what can only be described as a complex, turbulent event. New staff in particular are very vulnerable to the primitive defence mechanisms so characteristic of large groups, and need to be helped to understand them. I think it would be very difficult to supervise effectively without being a participant in this type of setting. Naturally I am also very dependent on feedback from my peers about myself in order to retain objectivity.

The focused groups that I supervise comprise a variety of small groups both in and out of the unit. These include an in-patient small group, a sex offenders group, an alcohol support group, an art therapy group (I am also an art therapist), a carers group for relatives of patients with Alzheimer's disease, a tranquilliser withdrawal group, a group for women, victims of sexual abuse and a weekly ward patient/staff meeting.

The community support groups are unique to the unit. These are groups that run on a weekly basis in the community for people with chronic mental illnesses. There are usually three therapists from different disciplines (doctors, social workers, occupational therapists and nurses are most commonly present). There are nine of these groups active and I supervise them weekly in a group setting. Supervision is invariably lively and stimulating.

Finally, I am responsible for organising a formal outpatient group-analytic group service. In the past, it was possible to recruit therapists from within the unit on a regular basis. This is a rarer event now because of the changes that have taken place in the unit.

SUMMARY

I hope that I have given some idea of the scope and variety of my work as a supervisor. This is of course only a portion of my duties as a group analyst working in the rare position of being employed full-time in the NHS. My future plans fall in line with the move towards care in the community. I am shortly to begin supervising staff working in a day centre for the ex-'long-stay' chronic population, now rehoused in the local town. I hope also to be closely involved in the setting up of a new day hospital next year. My involvement with the in-patient unit will probably then diminish. The unit will then have completed its metamorphosis from the old therapeutic community in which the post of group analyst was originally created.

Part II Group-analytic supervision in a psychiatric hospital

Morris Nitsun

Group-analytic supervision in the NHS needs to take account of the dramatic changes in mental health service delivery in the 1990s. The main elements of these changes are:

1 An escalating demand from the public for psychotherapeutic help;
2 The shrinking rather than expanding financial resources in public services; and
3 The competitive environment of health care in the UK, in which issues of cost-effectiveness and private contracting are uppermost.

These changes are reflected in the work of the Clinical Psychology Department of which I am head, and of which the adult section is based in a psychiatric hospital (Goodmayes). They also affect my clinical and supervisory functions as a group analyst in the same context. The combination of these functions is a challenging one and I believe there are important aspects to teach as well as to learn as a group analyst.

As a result of the increasing waiting list, mainly of outpatient referrals, in the Clinical Psychology Department, in the early 1990s we established a comprehensive programme of group treatments. At any one time, there might be ten groups running concurrently. Of these, most are short-term focused groups with more or less homogeneous membership. Examples include anxiety management groups, coping-with-depression groups, groups for adult survivors of childhood sexual abuse, and groups for women who are currently in abusive relationships. These are usually weekly groups that run for six to twelve weeks. They comprise up to ten participants and are frequently co-jointly run by two therapists. The reason for this is that the groups tend to have a psycho-educational component, requiring a certain amount of structured input from the therapists, and it is commonly found useful to share the task of teaching input, group facilitation, and process awareness. The groups are usually evaluated, with pre- and post-group measures which help to assess outcomes. On the whole, the groups are found to be effective and helpful to patients, whose comments and criticism provide valuable information as a basis for planning further groups.

These groups are complemented by the long-term psychotherapy groups of a group-analytic kind we run. These cater for more long-term, complex personality and interpersonal problems of the sort that do not fit into the short-term, focused groups. They are typically slow-open groups, carefully controlled for boundaries but open-ended and un-structured in terms of task. Membership is heterogeneous, with a load-ing towards serious psychological problems, including some psychiatric disorders, but not psychosis, drug addictions, or other severe forms of acting-out. The groups usually run for several years and are mainly conducted by a single therapist. Routine evaluation of these groups is not undertaken as it is thought to interfere with the group process. These groups can be difficult to implement and maintain in the NHS psy-chiatric hospital context: selection is difficult and more complex than for the short-term groups; patients evince greater ambivalence about joining such groups, including the long-term commitment required; and the groups themselves are fairly turbulent, with some degree of dis-satisfaction and dropping out on members' parts, although often with striking and profound life changes and personal development in those who stay the course.

The psychological mindedness ideally required for this sort of group is rather more difficult to come by in the cohort of typical NHS patients in the outer-London area in which I work than, for example, in private practice settings. Also, the group as a whole is a sensitive therapeutic instrument, strongly reactive to contextual changes in the host organ-isation and the NHS at large – probably because of the long period of dependence on the organisation and because of the psychological com-plexity and dynamic fluidity of the work undertaken in the group.

Here, then, are two different forms of group therapy provided con-currently in the same service. As I see it, the overall task that faces me in my combined role as head of department and group analyst is the provision of an integrative, holding framework within which both short-term and long-term groups, with their differing structures, value systems and benefits, can be run. Because of the large amount of administrative effort that goes into the setting up and implementing of the short-term group programme with its evaluation and feedback systems, and its emphasis on short-term benefits, there is a risk of the value of the long-term groups being lost or their fading into the background. A large part of my task is continually to reinforce the need for the extended and powerfully developmental therapeutic experience that may be gained in long-term groups. Equally, in the short-term groups, there is a need to understand the way the group process either facilitates or hinders the purpose of the group. Within the limited time span of these groups there are important issues about group boundaries, about group integration and development, about the stages that the group goes through (which are highly condensed in such a brief period), and about the recognition and handling of transference and counter-transference that inevitably occur, sometimes very intensely, in short-term groups. In other words, group-analytic understanding, with its emphasis on the group as a whole as a dynamic process, is relevant to those groups as well, sometimes crucially so. In sum, I see my role in the overall context of group treatment provision predominantly as maintaining the group-analytic perspective, an integrative perspective which can encompass and nurture the objectives of both short- and long-term groups.

This brings me to some illustrations of our work, outlining the differing but sometimes parallel processes in the two kinds of groups, and high-lighting the implications for the group-analytic supervisory role.

LONG-TERM GROUPS

The setting

As suggested above, I find issues about the setting extremely important in running long-term groups. By setting, I mean here the overall setting, which includes the physical environment and the organisational context in which the group takes place. Psychiatric hospitals are disturbing places, where latent fears of madness are easily aroused, compounded by actual psychiatric problems erupting into chaotic and fragmented behaviour. The unstructured nature of the analytic group, itself conducive to anxiety, intensifies projection onto and introjection from the external environment. Psychotherapy groups are vulnerable to the impact of outside influences, and I believe it is an essential goal to create a safe, holding environment for the group, a container for the disturbed feelings and imaginings that inevitably arise. This includes:

- Spatial factors such as a room which is sufficiently removed from the hurly-burly of the hospital and the impact of very disturbed psychiatric behaviour; and
- Temporal factors, such as ensuring a clear time-table of meetings, which avoids unplanned breaks or absences on the part of the conductor.

The qualities that Winnicott (1965) describes as part of the holding environment – consistency, regularity, and minimisation of impingement – are fundamental in creating a setting for long-term groups. It is also relevant that the group is recognised and supported within the department and the wider organisation – a parallel to the mother who needs her family's support in looking after her infant – and some effort is usefully expended on strengthening awareness of the existence and purpose of the group.

Selection

Given the scarcity of long-term psychotherapeutic help in the mental health field, there is a danger of very disturbed and unsuitable patients being dumped into analytic psychotherapy groups. I am less impressed than some by the capacity of groups to absorb all levels of disturbance and have seen destructive behaviour within and without the group seriously damage the integrity of the group. Also, essentially unmotivated patients who grudgingly accept group attendance tend to be a liability: they become a negative focus in the group and increase the drop-out rate, adding to doubt and demoralisation in the group.

The necessity of actively holding the group together in the psychiatric context is an on-going challenge and is aided by careful selection. I would highlight two criteria that I feel are underemphasised in selection for groups – bonding capacity and the group–object relation.

Bonding capacity, in line with the work of Bowlby (1988), refers to the capacity to form attachments *in* and *to* the group, and may be anticipated on the basis of an evaluation of patients' previous patterns of bonding. I recognise that patients entering group therapy by definition have problems in the area of attachment, but I regard it as to the advantage of the group to include some participants who have a reasonable capacity for bonding. This increases commitment and cohesiveness in the group: it also makes it possible to include some patients whose bonding capacity is more flawed but who may benefit from the nexus of attachment formed by the others.

The group–object relation is a term I use to describe patients' internal representation of groups, which is reflected in attitudes towards groups and characteristic ways of responding in group situations. The group–object relation merits close evaluation in the case of each prospective member, so as to accept individuals who may have difficulties in groups but not to the extent that the group will prove inimical to them or them to it. As psychiatric patients are known to have disturbed family and social histories, this issue is especially pertinent in the psychiatric context.

The process

I have previously written about the phenomenon of the anti-group (Nitsun 1991), describing an attitude of fear and dislike of groups which can be enacted in destructive ways in the group, including attacks on the group itself. This is implied in my comments above about the selection for groups. It is also highly relevant in considering and supervising the actual process of the group, in which anti-group reactions may undermine the therapeutic task.

While I see this as occurring potentially in all therapeutic groups, there may be a greater propensity for anti-group reactions in a group of psychiatric patients or, seen somewhat differently, in a group set in a psychiatric hospital. In these groups, there tends to be a marked degree of anxiety, often heightened rather than assuaged by being in a group, considerable psychopathology associated with hostility, rage, and hatred of the sort described by Kernberg (1991), and the operation of primitive defence mechanisms of projection, projective identification, fragmentation, or displacement. All of this can result in the group becoming an unsafe container, eliciting attacks which render it even more fragile.

In supervision, I consider the recognition and management of these processes very important in helping the conductor to deal with the anti-group. Techniques for dealing with hostility and instability in the group, as described by Gans (1989), Ormont (1984), and Hawkins (1986), are usefully considered, as are the conductor's own reactions to these phenomena. Feelings of despair and helplessness in the conductor are a sign of the anti-group at work, and supervision is vital in providing support and insight into this process.

SHORT-TERM GROUPS

On the surface, the tasks of the short-term group therapist are in direct contrast to those of the long-term group therapist. The aims of the brief group largely concern amelioration of immediate suffering and the provision of coping skills. The techniques are also different – the facilitator is likely to structure and direct the group, to set tasks, to suggest working in pairs or small sub-groups, and to encourage turn-taking in talking about individual problems – all at variance with the group-analytic emphasis on free group discussion and the emergence of unconscious themes from the group matrix. But short-term groups also evoke strong emotions, powerful mirroring processes, the developmental impact of beginning and ending the group, and often intense transference and counter-transference reactions. Understanding these phenomena in group-analytic terms and then relating this understanding to the specific group theme or task at hand is an important part of supervising groups of this kind.

An example of supervising a twelve-week group for women who had survived child sexual abuse illustrates some of these points.

> The group had a predetermined structure, in which each week started with feedback from individual members, followed by semi-didactic input from the therapist pair on a topic that had been agreed in advance with the participants (e.g. dealing with anger, disclosing the abuse) and ending with a period for reflecting on the application of these ideas. This approach had appeared to work well when, in the fourth session, participants' personal material started flooding the group, making it very difficult to carry out the structured tasks. The therapists found themselves in a dilemma. The material that came pouring out seemed extremely important and stopping it might mean destroying one of the few opportunities these women had ever had to talk openly about themselves. On the other hand, allowing a free flow would make it impossible to implement the original plans for the group.
>
> On the face of it, it seemed that it would be most therapeutic to open up the group space to the flow of personal material. However, in supervision, an important mirroring process in the group was identified. This concerned the issue of boundaries. These women's personal boundaries as children, and the generational boundaries between them and their parents, had been violated by the act of sexual abuse. In the group, their outpourings were threatening to undermine the boundaries created by the therapists

for the purpose of the group task. If the therapists yielded to this process, they might be colluding in a repetition of an earlier traumatic invasion of boundaries. If, on the other hand, they stuck to their programme, enabling free discussion but within the time period originally set, they might be affirming boundaries in a way that could be safe and containing to the women. The therapists decided to share their dilemma with the participants, not interpreting the unconscious dynamics, but emphasising the group task. The women agreed strongly to keeping to the structured format and to limiting the time spent on personal revelations. This itself seemed to be a salutary move: involving the participants in the decision helped to give them a sense of control when the abuse they had suffered had robbed them of personal control.

Another issue concerned the 'goodness' of the group. The therapists felt a mixture of pleasure and uneasiness about the very positive atmosphere in the group. Although much of the content of the material was very disturbing, there was a high degree of commitment and involvement in the group, with considerable mutual support. The therapists had expected a more difficult, chaotic group, with the abuse being enacted in symbolic form in the group. They had also expected to be attacked and undermined as therapists. None of this materialised in the group. If anything, the participants seemed to put the therapists on a pedestal and admire them from afar.

In supervision, the therapists expressed their puzzlement at this highly constructive group, given the participants' destructive early life experiences. Where was 'the bad object'? Was some form of splitting going on, in which all the bad was repressed or disassociated in some way, perhaps relegated to the past? Would this all catch up with members after the group had ended, resulting in a traumatic negative post-therapeutic reaction? The supervisor discussed with the therapists possible ways of intervening to evoke greater intragroup ambivalence and hostility. But the more this was discussed, the more it was felt to be wrong. An underlying principle gradually emerged – the fact that these women were able to have a good experience in the group should be seen as an achievement, not a failure. Further, their idealisation of the therapists could be seen not as defensive but as a healthy need to idealise parental figures in a way that they had not been able to do before: the therapists represented the unsullied, undamaged parts of themselves – and their parents – that they were hoping to recover through their participation in the group. To challenge this in a short-term group, without the opportunity for further working-through, might be experienced by participants as a painful rejection of the hopeful, idealising parts of themselves.

This group is not unusual in illustrating the powerful communication that can occur in a short-term, focused group. In fact, I have been struck by the irony that in long-term groups, where communication is the essential therapeutic medium, the unstructured nature of the group often elicits silence, resistance, and defensive communication, whereas in structured groups, where limited time is allowed for personal exploration, communication can be unstoppable. Possibly, the limited time available in each group and the overall brevity of the therapy endeavour exerts a pressure to communicate which is absent in long-term groups. Another example is a communications group I ran myself. In the 'personal time' period in one session, participants' exploration of their earlier lives produced deeply affecting material.

One member (A) described the early, painful parental rejection he had experienced which he said he had never fully revealed before. A female member (B) reacted with considerable sensitivity to him, but he appeared not to notice. This was in keeping with his tendency to look away in the midst of an empathic communication – a feature that had been identified when members' communication patterns had been analysed. When this was pointed out in the current interaction, (A) made direct eye contact with (B). She was very moved and reached out further emotionally to him. In turn, he was very moved. The whole group was caught in a moment of intense attunement that provided a spontaneous corrective to the neglect and misattunement that had characterised their emotional lives. The focus on communication and the structured nature of the group had helped to create a valuable encounter for all concerned.

DISCUSSION

These are humbling experiences. They have challenged some of my underlying assumptions about therapeutic work in groups. One of these assumptions is that group therapy needs to be long-term in order to be therapeutic and developmental, another is that material of intrapsychic significance is likely to merge only in an unstructured group. On the contrary, it appears that structure and a clear task focus may provide safety and containment in a way that makes it possible to take the risk of opening up. Having said this, it is equally clear to me that the dynamic processes in short-term groups are not essentially different from those in long-term groups: rather, they appear in more condensed form. This makes the group-analytic perspective a particularly valuable one in the supervision of short-term groups.

The space for therapists to explore their personal reactions to the group, to examine the mirroring that occurs at various levels of the group, and to consider the continuing link between content and process, all confirm the value of group-analytic supervision as a holding frame for the brevity and intensity of the short-term group. This parallels my view that in long-term group work, the provision of a holding environment – all the way from the physical setting to the availability of supervisory support – is a crucial requirement. In both cases, the regular, supportive nature of supervision symbolises the framework of a holding environment. This is essential in the psychiatric setting, where fragmentation and failures of containment are at the core of individuals' lives.

The changing shape of psychotherapeutic services in the late twentieth century offers important challenges to the group analyst and the group-analytic supervision process: challenges, as suggested earlier, both to teaching and learning.

REFERENCES – PART II

Bowlby, J. (1988) *A Secure Base*, London: Routledge.
Gans, J.S. (1989) 'Hostility in group psychotherapy', *International Journal of Group Psychotherapy* 39(4): 499–516.
Hawkins, D.K. (1986) 'Understanding reactions to group instability in psychotherapy groups', *International Journal of Group Psychotherapy* 36: 241–259.
Kernberg, I. (1991) 'The psychopathology of hatred', *Journal of the American Psychoanalytic Association* 39 (Supplement): 209–238.
Nitsun, M. (1991) 'The anti-group: destructive forces in the group and their therapeutic potential', *Group Analysis* 24(1): 7–20.
Nitsun, M. (1994) *The Anti-Group: The Dialectics of the Creative and Destructive in Groups*, London: Routledge.
Ormont, L.R. (1984) 'The leader's role in dealing with aggression in groups', *International Journal of Group Psychotherapy* 34: 553–572.
Winnicott, D.W. (1965) *The Theory of the Parent–Infant Relationship in the Maturational Processes and the Facilitating Environment*, New York: International University Press.

Part III Supervision in therapeutic communities

Jane Knowles

Group work in a therapeutic community (TC) takes many forms. There are the fun groups, the purely practical 'Who is not taking their turn at washing up?' groups, psychodrama, drama therapy and art groups, and much social interaction between each of the organised and scheduled activities. In the Winterbourne community at Fair Mile in Berkshire these groups are threaded together to form a cohesive pattern by an underlying structure of small- and large-group analysis.

The large groups consist of all the staff and clients, often amounting to 35 people, the small groups of between four to nine clients and two staff members. One of the staff members, usually the most experienced, is designated as leader of each of the small groups, while the other staff member is seen by staff and clients alike as the trainee co-leader. Usually their on-the-job training within the community is backed up by further external training, but most are not group analysts.

Within the structure of a TC, staff are more exposed to the clients than in a stranger outpatient group. They spend each and every day together in a variety of settings as well as the 75 minutes a day they spend in small-group analysis and the hour twice a week in large-group analysis. This means that theory has to be expanded to fit the context and that supervision has to reflect that expansion. Clients know their therapists both as workers and as private individuals. We write reports and letters together, work alongside each other in the kitchen, struggle to improve our table tennis together, all report about our out-of-hours lives in 'weekend news' on a Monday morning and give straightforward explanations for staff behaviour such as absences. Little is truly opaque. Despite this, transference flourishes and because of it clients, especially the more experienced community clients, are just as likely to spot our counter-transference as we are.

Understanding the importance of shifting attention from figure to background and back again is of central importance in helping individuals change in this organisational structure. The main role of the supervisor is to have an overview of the working of the community which allows him or her to gain a dynamic understanding of the many layers of psychological work in progress at any one time. In this sense it is supervision of many concentric circles, small group within large group within community. Sometimes this might, in metaphor, feel like a uterine home, within a nursery, within a family, at others it feels like a family with adolescents struggling within society. The whole community can shift the metaphoric focus within a few hours and often does so several times a week.

To help staff cope with the flood of material, the ever present threat of chaotic acting-out and the danger that the most vulnerable community member, be that a member of staff or a client at any moment of time, may act like a lightning conductor for the wealth of intense emotions present, a supervisor needs to be both involved enough to understand staff pressures while also external enough to gain perspective.

On the Winterbourne unit we achieve this by employing ex-staff members to return on a sessional basis as supervisors. Their past experience coupled with their capacity to have an oversight of the unit from outside is invaluable. We have separate supervisors for the small and large groups although both regularly attend each other's supervision sessions. This honours the fact that the small and large group represent different experiences in which different community members hold sway and bring forth very different material. Such supervision occurs on a weekly basis, as does the staff sensitivity group which also has an external leader and immediately precedes large-group supervision. This arrangement has the benefit that much counter-transference material has already emerged and been acknowledged by individual staff members prior to formal supervision.

Alongside the weekly formal supervision sessions, group leaders meet together each day after small groups for immediate feedback. Twice a week, as consultant, I attend a brief pre-lunch meeting for all staff which allows for immediate large-group feedback. This more informal supervision is seen as just as important as the formal sessions in allowing ventilation of staff feelings and exploration of dynamics necessary for day-to-day healthy functioning of the unit.

All supervision is verbal; groups are not written up, videoed or audio-taped in any way. However, each of the three small groups has an opportunity to feed back to the unit as a whole once every three months. This is achieved in the context of the large group with a community member from another small group 'in the chair'. Gestalt techniques are often used to enhance this process, for instance, 'Pretend your group is a garden. What role are you each playing?' Community members and staff take an active part in feeding back to the group at the end of these sessions.

Supervision of the therapeutic community ethos is achieved in business meetings in which staff and clients participate. The boundary between what is a community decision and what decisions remain in the domain of the staff has to be constantly monitored in this arena. In this way supervision is always mirroring the therapeutic work in the community, lying in the concentric circles of activity, and moving from small group, to large group, to community and back again in the course of a week. As the contextual focus shifts so too does our focus from individual to group and back to individual.

Chapter 8

St Bartholomew's Hospital psychotherapy service

Vivienne Cohen

St Bartholomew's Hospital, whose Medical School is a constituent college of the University of London, comprises a large prestigious National Health Service teaching hospital in the City of London and a sister hospital, Bart's Homerton, sited in Hackney in the East End of London. The joint hospitals service the very large commuting population of the City, about 350,000 people from shop assistants to bankers, a local community of about 100,000, and the population of Hackney, the most economically deprived borough in the UK, with a population approaching 200,000.

There is a large Department of Psychological Medicine, including all major sub-specialties, with twenty-one consultants, including a Professor and many Senior Lecturers. The Psychotherapy Unit is relatively small in established posts – one Senior Lecturer and Consultant in Dynamic Psychotherapy, and one Consultant in Cognitive Psychotherapy, both of whom respectively work closely with a Clinical Nurse Specialist in Dynamic Psychotherapy and a Clinical Nurse Specialist in Behaviour Therapy; the posts of Consultant in Cognitive Therapy and Clinical Nurse Specialist in Dynamic Psychotherapy are both recently created. Notwithstanding the small establishment, the dynamic psychotherapy service is one of the best and most extensive in the country, with a reputation locally, regionally, and even nationally, for high calibre treatment and a high rate of acceptance of referrals. It is widely recognised in North East Thames as a 'hidden' (i.e. unofficial) regional specialty.

The majority of referrals for dynamic psychotherapy come from general (family) practitioners and from the psychiatrists and other staff of the Department of Psychological Medicine. Some patients are referred by psychiatrists and psychotherapists outside the hospital, a few come directly from physicians and surgeons of the joint hospitals, and a number from counsellors and Community Psychiatric Nurses (with the agreement of the patient's general practitioner).

The backbone of the service is analytic group psychotherapy. The first analytic group at Bart's was conducted by Dr S. H. Foulkes, then a member of the staff, and began on 30 November 1946. On his appointment to the Maudsley Hospital in 1950 group psychotherapy disappeared from Bart's until the appointment of the author in 1964. With the establishment in 1971 of the Institute of Group Analysis, trainee group analysts were offered the opportunity of conducting a group under supervision at Bart's in an honorary capacity and it became possible to extend the psychotherapy service, first in 1972 with the assistance of one trainee, and now in 1993 with twelve trainees and graduates conducting analytic groups, all on honorary contracts; a further five groups are conducted by members of the Department. Because of their relative inexperience, psychiatric trainees treat only individual patients, and are discouraged from conducting a group except as co-therapist to an experienced group analyst (see Figure 8.1).

The Qualifying Course of the Institute of Group Analysis requires its trainees to conduct a weekly group of mixed adult outpatients who are strangers to each other for a minimum of two years (from 1993, two and a half years). All but the very first Qualifying Course student to conduct a group at Bart's have continued for longer and some have found the patient groups so rewarding that they have continued for five, six or even eight years. This is partly attributable to the high calibre of patients referred to the Consultant Psychotherapist, but the role of the consultant in providing support, back-up and supervision is crucial. The opportunity of conducting a group at Bart's has always been highly prized by Qualifying Course students.

At any one time there are fourteen to seventeen long-term, slow-open, analytic groups in the department, of which all but one are of the kind described above. One is a special group for women sexually abused in childhood. In addition, there are closed, short-life groups for selected patients attending the day-care unit.

Eight to ten of the long-term groups are supervised by the Consultant Psychotherapist in a weekly group supervision seminar. A group analyst is employed for one session a week to supervise the short-life groups at the day-care unit and to conduct a seminar attended by four of the group conductors. The group for women sexually abused in childhood is supervised fortnightly by the consultant. For three group conductors, changes in their work schedules have necessitated separate supervisory arrangements.

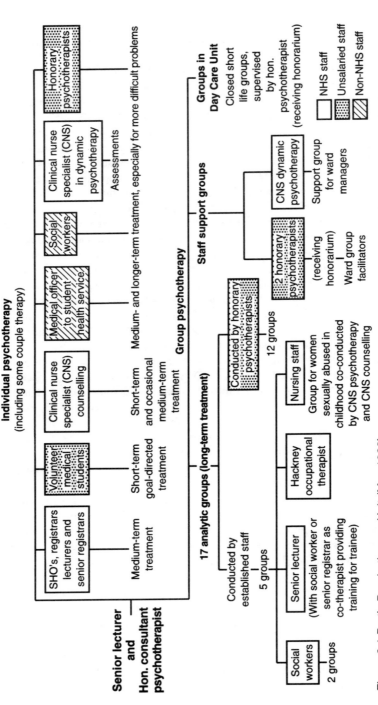

Individual psychotherapy
(including some couple therapy)

SHO's, registrars lecturers and senior registrars	Volunteer medical students	Clinical nurse specialist (CNS) counselling	Medical officer to student health service	Social workers	Clinical nurse specialist (CNS) in dynamic psychotherapy	Honorary psychotherapists
Medium-term treatment	Short-term goal-directed treatment	Short-term and occasional medium-term treatment				

Medium- and longer-term treatment, especially for more difficult problems

Assessments

**Senior lecturer
and
Hon. consultant
psychotherapist**

Group psychotherapy

17 analytic groups (long-term treatment)

Conducted by established staff
5 groups

Social workers	Senior lecturer
2 groups	(With social worker or senior registrar as co-therapist providing training for trainee)

Hackney occupational therapist	Nursing staff
	Group for women sexually abused in childhood co-conducted by CNS psychotherapy and CNS counselling

Conducted by honorary psychotherapists
12 groups

Staff support groups

2 honorary psychotherapists	CNS dynamic psychotherapy
(receiving honorarium) Ward group facilitators	Support group for ward managers

Groups in Day Care Unit

Closed short life groups, supervised by hon. psychotherapist (receiving honorarium)

Legend:
☐ NHS staff
▨ Unsalaried staff
▧ Non-NHS staff

Figure 8.1 Bart's Psychotherapy Unit (May 1993)

At the beginning, supervision of each student by the consultant was organised individually, at mutually convenient times, but as the number grew, it was agreed in 1978 that group supervision was preferable and that a supervision seminar should be established despite the difficulties of arranging it. This seminar has been running continuously for fifteen years and, since the author's retirement in 1993, has been maintained by her successor.

The seminar group meets for one and a half hours at midday once a week; the members sit in an informal circle in the consultant's office, which also serves as a group room. There are usually seven to ten conductors present, the majority being trainees or graduates of the Institute of Group Analysis; latterly one or two students from another training organisation have been admitted. Group conductors are expected to keep notes of each group session (recorded as soon as possible after the session) and to maintain an attendance chart but reporting is informal and reading from notes is unusual. Any urgent problems are dealt with first; this frequently leads to extensive discussion, and the conductor who asks for a 'quickie' may very often need half an hour or more of the group's attention to deal fruitfully with the problem. Except in the case of new trainees, a pattern of presentation has evolved in which the account of events tends to be quite sharply focused, partly perhaps because of the very large size of the seminar group (in some ways too large) but it has also proved to be a model which is an invaluable 'honing' exercise for all participants.

A very special culture has evolved over the long period, fifteen years, of the seminar's existence. The members of the group know each other well; they are colleagues, friends, occasionally patients in the same analytic group and, in other settings, sometimes rivals. Together they have weathered the vicissitudes of working in an often troubled NHS setting, on an honorary contract with the further inevitable burden of feeling marginalised through their unusual hours (early morning or evening) and the part-time nature of their work. The seminar is crucial in creating and maintaining a sense of corporate identity. Most of the discussion in the supervisory session takes place between the conductors, and their wide range of knowledge and competence, from first-year students to graduates of substantial experience and skill, adds richness and deepens the scope of the seminar and helps to ensure that competitiveness does not become destructive. These factors have led to a relaxed, robust, cohesive and containing group, highly supportive yet able to be confronting where appropriate, and the group members have a profound understanding and respect for each individual's personal approach, strengths and weaknesses.

All members of the seminar who are still trainees are in concurrent supervision at their training institutes. This has its advantages but sometimes leads to problems which are of two types – one is a split transference towards the two supervisors, one becoming the all-good parent and the other all-bad. The other is the dilemma of receiving conflicting advice from the two supervisors or from the two seminar groups. The former problem needs interpreting and is then usually taken to the student's personal therapy; the latter requires the supervisees to learn to stand on their own feet and make their own decisions and choices. The supervisor has an important role to play in facilitating the resolution of these situations but where there is respect between the two supervisors, the difficulties are only transitory.

Particularly impressive is the group's capacity to bring to light, disentangle, and analyse problems of counter-transference. The supervision seminar is not, and should not be seen as, a therapeutic group and the conductor's personal problems belong in his or her own therapy, but such is the safety of the seminar that supervisees on occasion may share very intimate material, such as that which follows, usually with considerable personal gain.

> Three or four weeks before the author's retirement from Bart's a talented group conductor who was in the fourth year of conducting his group had just begun a session when the silence was shattered by a series of explosions. Only a few weeks previously, there had been a massive explosion in the City of London and although on this occasion it was almost immediately discovered that this was only a fireworks display, terror and fear of destruction had gripped the group, including the conductor. A group member, Anne, broke the helpless silence saying that she had felt a sense of powerlessness and panic which had brought back to her the horrific time when she was young and her mother had suddenly packed a bag for her and her sister and had arranged to despatch them to a father whose whereabouts they did not know and with whom they had had sparse contact. The theme was taken up by another patient who, as if it were an amusing anecdote, described the time when his mother had stood him and his brother on the parapet of a bridge over the Thames with the intention of pushing both to their deaths – an act from which she was only deflected by the intervention of a passer-by.

At the next session Anne announced indignantly that she had been angry all the week because the conductor had not heard what she had said about the terror she and her sister had experienced and had cut across her to give his attention to the other patient: 'If this is what being a good father is, it's crap, and you are crap'.

The following week, at supervision, the conductor presented these events in a detached monotone, quite unlike his usual manner, adding that he had, indeed, not heard what Anne had said the previous week. Another member of the seminar remarked on his expressionless voice, commenting that for some weeks he had lacked lustre in the supervision group. The author at this point asked, 'Did you say you hadn't heard what Anne had said about being thrown out of the house?' The conductor then painfully and movingly shared with the seminar an associated memory of his own. Gulping, his voice cracking, he described how, during the war, his mother had assured him that she had sufficient poison to kill both of them should the Germans land. The tears flowed and he sobbed in a sudden access of grief over his mother, his 'murder', her death and, most immediate, over the consultant's imminent departure. Afterwards he said he felt 'whole' again, and the next session of his group flowed effortlessly.

Although attendance at a seminar is obligatory for group conductors, changes in the work schedule of a conductor occasionally preclude his or her continued participation, and individual supervision has to be arranged. In unusual circumstances, individual supervision may be arranged from the outset. The most immediately obvious and striking difference in such situations is how much less lively the presentation usually becomes. Perhaps a larger audience stirs all of us into a more sparkling response. The creative input and support of fellow supervisees is a major loss, especially on those occasions where it is necessary to be confrontative with a trainee of vulnerable personality. On the other hand, with a very sensitive trainee it is sometimes possible to deal more freely with counter-transference issues than in a group.

The Bart's seminar group has become a powerful and peerless training tool with a unique culture quite unlike, for example, that of the author's own supervision seminars at the IGA which, however good, never quite achieve the same creative quality. The fact that at Bart's there is no reporting, feedback or official monitoring of the conductors' progress results in less tension and allows for a much greater degree of personal freedom in the seminar. Supervisees remark that it feels less competitive. The sense of shared experience and of belonging is strong and invigorating and there is very solid mutual respect.

Not without reason are the Bart's group conductors affectionately known in the Department of Psychological Medicine as 'the groupies'.

Chapter 9

Supervision in trans-cultural block training courses

Harold L. Behr
Lisbeth E. Hearst
Per A. Føyn
Felix Schwarzenbach

Part I Supervisors

Harold L. Behr and Lisbeth E. Hearst

The London Institute of Group Analysis has developed a unique model of training in which the trainee's personal group analysis (conducted in twice-weekly patient groups), supervision and theory teaching, are held in relation to one another in a triadic structure. This model has also provided the prototype for those training courses which the Institute has set up and has been conducting in other countries in blocks of time lasting for several days and separated by fairly long intervals, a format known as 'Block Training'. The time and space setting of these block sessions differs from the continuous weekly training experience of the trainees on the London Qualifying Course. A modification of content and technique is therefore required, while at the same time maintaining the triadic structure and ensuring that the standard of training is kept at a high level.

Probably the most important modification is that of the therapy groups in which the trainee is placed. In block training these groups are made up of trainees only, and in this sense are homogeneous groups. The structures of the course allow for less choice in the constitution of the group than is the case in the mixed trainee and patient groups of the classical training course, but as far as possible the trainee groups also contain the widest possible span of age, personality, familial and professional background. Close social and professional relationships outside the group are avoided in composing these groups, as they are on the Continuous Qualifying Course. The supervision groups tend to be larger on the Block Training Programme – up to twelve members – than those of the Continuous Qualifying Course, which have four, or at the most five members in the ongoing training.

The Block Courses meet for three to five days at a time; each day comprises up to four small group sessions, one large group session, one theory seminar and one supervision group, and these follow one another in rapid succession. Because of this structure the trainees encounter their group analyst in a variety of roles throughout the day, and though supervision and therapy are clearly separated into different groups conducted by different group analysts, the close proximity in time and space creates a transference situation which must be understood and evaluated in the context of this special setting. The rapid change between different kinds of groups – small therapy groups, supervision groups, theory seminar groups, large groups, and organisational plenary groups – means that there is a constant change of roles for trainees and therapists. The trainees are required to sustain the movement between regression in the therapy group and didactic functioning in the theory and supervision sessions (Balmer 1993).

As the trainer moves from one group setting to another, a change of posture is called for – a different kind of listening and relating – in quick succession throughout the days of the training block. The close juxtaposition of therapy and supervision in particular affords a rich opportunity for trainees to examine issues arising in supervision which have led to counter-transference distortions, working on them in the therapy and making connections between the trainees' personal experience of therapy and the professional conducting of their training groups. A similar interconnectedness is achieved on the Continuous Training Programme but inevitably with less intensity and immediacy, due to the wider time scatter throughout the week between supervision and therapy sessions.

These intense emotional experiences in the blocks are followed by long intervals during which neither the therapy group nor the group analyst are available. Trainees are therefore supervised in a rhythm which is not synchronous with the therapy groups which they themselves conduct as part of the training experience. Like their counterparts on the Continuous Course, they are required to conduct their training groups at weekly intervals, and long periods of time elapse during which no weekly supervision is available. The supervision session can therefore take place long after an immediate problem arising in the trainee's group has occurred.

The weekly rhythm of the trainee's training group superimposed on the much less frequent rhythm of supervision can at times be experienced as a deprivation, or even as an act of emotional violence perpetrated by the supervisor on the supervisee.

In the first supervision group of a block, the group seemed pleased to be meeting again after an interval of three months. The members of the group were asked who wanted to report in that session and who in the two following ones, and what the reports would concern themselves with. (This is the procedure on this course by which the work of the supervision group in each block is determined.) On this occasion the supervisor noticed a reluctance to stake a claim, noticeably different from previous supervision sessions where group members were always eager to be allocated space. Eventually the programme was drawn up and the first report began. The subject was of general interest and applicable to many trainees present, yet the presentation was lifeless and hesitant, and the discussion strained. The supervisor felt disappointed, let down by the group, and somehow separate from it. This was a novel feeling for her in this supervision group, and she decided to halt the programme and submit these feelings to the group. There followed a silence, and then a woman said: 'I too feel let down, I don't know what about and why'. A man told the group that he had been waiting for the supervision session – he needed it 'for dear life' in his group work. At this, a woman began to cry silently. The group and the supervisor were startled by this: it had never before happened in a supervision session. Then someone told the group that the woman who was crying had had a bereavement in her family. Others seemed to know of this also. (In spite of the rules requiring group members to abstain from socialising outside the group and to observe confidentiality, information in block courses travels fast, and is readily available to course members.) The woman concerned became agitated, and said that she could and did deal with her bereavement in her therapy group; but she felt angry and let down, because a patient in her training group had had a near-fatal accident. The group had been terribly upset, and she herself felt inadequate to help the group bear the experience and work it through. 'And you' (meaning the supervisor and the supervision group) 'weren't there when I needed you most. I was left to deal with it alone.' The mood in the supervision group now changed from restraint and near-apathy to engaged participation. The spaced-out supervision timetable was, of course, known to the participants, and they had been working in this mode for a considerable time. But only in that session did the negative emotional impact come to light: namely, feelings of desertion, lack of guidance, helplessness, and a fear that these might result in a near-fatality or death.

Occasionally the reaction to the relatively wide time gap between supervision sessions takes the form of a stoical self-sufficiency, a determination to 'go it alone' and the tendency to withdraw emotionally from the supervision group and withhold material. When material is presented, it is sometimes packaged in the form of a résumé which, if allowed to go unchallenged, deprives the trainee of the opportunity for thinking about the group in a more reflective, free-associative way. Where a crisis within the group has arisen in the interval between sessions, the trainee may be apprehensive about criticism of the way in which the group was managed.

A trainee became alarmed at the rate at which new group members were dropping out after only a few sessions. The supervision group established that this had been a problem for several months, originating even earlier than the previous block supervision, when he had declined an opportunity for an in-depth presentation on the grounds that his group was 'going quite well'.

The trainee's material helped the group to construct a picture of his training group consisting of a core of depressed, withdrawn, angry men who, along with the therapist himself, were making it difficult for any new member to feel accepted in the group. It turned out that most of the drop-outs were women, and that the therapist had made hardly any efforts to retrieve them, but had adopted a stubborn, 'shut-off' attitude to those who he felt 'could not be bothered to make the commitment to attend regularly'. His self-image was one of caring and empathy, and the supervision group helped him to get in touch with an angry, rejecting, uncaring side of himself which he had rationalised as 'strictly holding the boundary of the group'. Further exploration disclosed a silent, withholding style of conducting, which he justified on the basis of not wishing to encourage too much dependency and regression by being too forthcoming.

The link with supervision was highlighted in a dialogue between supervisor and trainee in which it became clear that the infrequency of supervision sessions was reinforcing the trainee's basic philosophy that a withholding approach to therapy was an effective means of counteracting strong dependency needs. The trainee spontaneously began to reflect on his own isolated childhood in a small community, where his memory was of his father, a naval officer, whom he idealised, and who was frequently away from home, and a depressed, withdrawn mother towards whom he felt a mixture of anger and compassion. The supervisor felt that the trainee was moving into a more therapeutic mode and encouraged the trainee to continue to work on this material in his own therapy group, and to stay with the task of looking at the drop-out problem in his supervision group. Many avenues were opened up in the peer group discussion, and over the ensuing months the trainee's style became more relaxed and generous, and he achieved a more stable, balanced group.

'As a rule, the intervals between sessions in block training are well sustained by the supervisees. It seems that the supervision group becomes internalised by the members of the group and in this way experienced as always available' (Reik 1993: 158). Group members often report that when puzzled or worried by an event or a patient in the training group, they would wonder what the supervision group would advise were it present. The supervisor can also experience increased anxiety and may wonder whether patients are dropping out of the training groups, or whether all is well with the groups and patients during the intervals. There may be a heightened and often unrealistic sense of responsibility, in spite of adequate support structures and local professionals with ultimate clinical responsibility having been carefully arranged beforehand (Marrone 1993).

To offset the difficulties created by the time gap, a model of peer group supervision has evolved in which the trainees gather at weekly or fortnightly intervals between blocks, and function as a mutual supervision group along group-analytic lines. Formulations developed by peer groups in relation to a particular training group are sometimes brought to the block supervision session as part of the material to be looked at. Peer groups provide a powerful corrective influence on idiosyncratic technique and counter-transferential distortion, and any collusive group dynamic developing in the core group is easily identified and addressed during the weekend block supervision sessions. In practice, however, this hardly arises and the peer groups restore a rhythm to the supervision which is no longer significantly at odds with the training group sessions. Where trainees gather from far-flung parts of the country and practical obstacles make it difficult to assemble at frequent intervals, a model of telephone supervision has been developed which enables the peer group to confer through a telephone conference.

The personal emotional content brought out during a supervision session does of course belong to the therapy group where it can be worked with in depth. It is important to keep the distinction between therapy and supervision clear and consistent. It is, however, equally essential to discern and address emotional states which, if unrecognised and unaddressed, interfere with the task of the group, which is to facilitate an ever-deepening and widening understanding of the groups which trainees conduct, and an increasing skill in their clinical work as group analysts. If unconscious transference phenomena interfere with this functioning, they must be addressed and analysed. The supervisor uses the same tools in this task as does the group analyst, namely, observation, empathy, linking, and the counter-transference experienced by the supervisor within the supervision group. In block supervision this task has to be clearly perceived and urgently addressed since the long intervals between blocks do not allow for postponement.

The modified setting also influences the content of the sessions. The material presented is rarely that of one session: rather, there is pressure to do what the word 'supervision' originally meant: to oversee, look at the sum total, at trends, developments, overall meaning. This process has the advantage for the supervisee of seeing development, blockages and danger signals more easily and clearly, and it avoids being too influenced by single events in the group.

The large size of the supervision group makes it impossible for all members to present their groups every time. This makes it important to stress the relevance of each presentation to every member, by paying special attention to the feelings aroused by the presentation and the reactions of the supervision group to the presentation and the presenter. Presentations have to be much more focused, attempts to deliver long and detailed accounts of the history of the group or individual histories of group members are discouraged, and a culture is created in which either the raw material of sessions is presented or where specific issues are focused on that bring out the feelings and experience of the trainee, rather than a condensed or encapsulated summary of the material. Emotional interaction and engagement of the supervision group is achieved by an extensive use of the counter-transference, by which the supervision group acquires insight into the dynamic phenomena of the group being presented. It is true that all supervision proceeds on this basis, but the fact that overviews, often extending over a large number of sessions, are being presented makes the counter-transference phenomena very vivid in a figure–ground constellation (Olivieri-Larsson 1993).

A relatively inexperienced group conductor presented an inpatient group which he was conducting in the hospital in which he was a Registrar. His presentation concentrated on a 'male patient' (as he called him) whose behaviour in the group he found puzzling and disconcerting. He gave the supervision group a detailed account of this patient's history and previous treatment, and he spoke with concern and engagement. The supervision group enquired about childhood relationships and events in this patient's history: the atmosphere resembled that of a psychiatric case conference. The supervisor pointed this out and wondered where the group was in all this: the supervision group seemed to treat the presentation as if the therapy were taking place within a dyad. A woman member then reflected that she had altogether forgotten the group, and had become quite fascinated with the relationship between the presenter (the Registrar) and his patient. Two other group members confirmed that this had been so for them also. Someone else observed that it was surely legitimate to concentrate on one patient; after all, therapy was there for the patient, not for the group. The group was only a means to an end. The presenter agreed enthusiastically, but then became thoughtful and told the group that he felt competent in individual psychotherapy, but uncertain, and at times deskilled, in group psychotherapy. 'I would understand the psychodynamics of the patient if we were alone. In the group, I am puzzled. I wish I had him in individual therapy.'

The supervision group comprised members at different stages of training. The more experienced group therapists recalled their feelings of insecurity in the early stages of conducting groups, and compared them with their present sense of being able to follow their groups. Someone gave a case vignette in which her group had worked optimally; she described the unconscious linking in the matrix, and the resulting illumination of the material brought by one patient in the group. The Registrar was now able to explore his sense of being incompetent, but also felt understood and empathised with within the supervision group. He recalled that his group had withdrawn from him and the patient and had 'left us to ourselves'. It had been strangely unsatisfactory. He felt he now understood himself and the group better, and he seemed interested in, and animated by, the group process in that session.

This supervision session took place in the context of a block training course in a country with a long tradition of psychoanalytic treatment, but hardly any of group psychotherapy or group analysis. It is difficult for the trainees to set up training groups, because prospective patients ask for individual psychotherapy and are resistant to coming into groups. They see it as second best; one is 'put into a group' when the therapist has no vacancy for individual therapy, or because it is 'cheaper'. The psychotherapists themselves subconsciously share this attitude in spite of having joined an arduous and expensive training in order to become group analysts. They have acquired their professional identity in a highly individualistic society and it has become part of their professional culture, undetected by them. There is therefore an emotional collusion with the patients in the denigration of group psychotherapy. This has to become conscious and addressed in supervision. When it has been worked through, the trainees' groups become more dynamic and analytically potent, and the trainee conductor experiences an intensification of interest and enjoyment in conducting. This newly found confidence in group analysis emerges in the initial interviews with prospective group patients and helps them to entrust themselves to group analysis, thus helping to change the therapeutic environment and culture.

A different set of issues arises in a culture where psychodynamic mental health care is dominated by medicine and psychiatry and where trainees are largely drawn from this pool. The tendency to structure therapeutic groups along prescriptive lines and to take on dual or even multiple roles in relation to group members can be a powerful dynamic and has to be addressed both in supervision and therapy. Psychiatrists practising in relatively small communities may find themselves having to play an active part in the management of their group members through prescribing of medication, signing of sick leave forms, writing letters on behalf of group members, and monitoring patients' progress in psychiatric outpatient clinics, as well as functioning as the patient's group analyst. The pressure to act in these powerful ways comes not only from the trainee but from the patient and the training group itself, and is condoned to an extent by the wider community. However, many of the dilemmas presented in this guise within supervision can be reframed in group-analytic terms and successfully addressed, often with the help of a nucleus of understanding peers who are in the strong position of being able to speak for the host community and point out to a trainee the defensive characteristics of the wish to retain overall management of a group member's care. Realistic solutions to these management problems are usually found, and in the process, group-analytic thinking will permeate beyond the training course into the wider network as colleagues outside of the course become aware of the possibility of alternative ways of managing patients.

Another discernible cultural component in supervision comes from the established teaching methods in schools and higher education. These have an hierarchical and authoritarian orientation, in which the student trainee expects instruction and clear, unequivocal guidelines. In such a culture, the supervisor is looked upon as the source of knowledge and skill, which the student defers to and complies with. This is even more so when the trainers are seen to come from a prestigious institute abroad, flying in and out for each block of training. The opposite is also true: there are cultures where students exercise a high degree of consumer choice in their training, which is apt to deny the disparity of knowledge and experience between trainer and trainee. For the purpose of super-vision, this culturally induced attitude is probably closer to the optimal supervision process in group analysis, which is a subtle sharing process, in which the supervisee, the supervisor, and the supervision group are in unconscious and conscious communication with one another (Sharpe and Blackwell 1987). It is in the matrix of this communication that the supervisees gain understanding of the group and individual processes, and their own role in them. Hierarchical and authoritarian expectations tend to stand in the way of such communication, and when they occur, they should be made conscious and addressed in the supervision group. This may be a slow process of adaptation and change. The supervisor must hold on to the group-analytic attitude, which stresses that the group supervisor, like the group conductor, is a member of the supervision group rather than its instructor, and must function as such.

REFERENCES – PART I

Balmer, R. (1993) 'Therapeutic factors: meeting them in block training', *Group Analysis* 26(2): 139–145.
Marrone, M. (1993) 'Analytic group therapy in block sessions. An experience in Milan', *Group Analysis* 26(2): 147–155.
Olivieri-Larsson, R. (1993) 'Superego conflicts in supervision', *Group Analysis* 26(2): 169–176.
Reik, H. (1993) 'The creative capacity of boundaries in block training', *Group Analysis* 26(2): 157–161.
Sharpe, M. and Blackwell, D. (1987) 'Creative supervision through student involvement', *Group Analysis* 20(3): 195–208.

Part II Supervisee: experiences from five years of the block course for group-analytic training in Norway

Per A. Føyn

> I'm Nobody! Who are you?
> Are You – Nobody – too?
> Then there's a pair of us!
> Don't tell! They'd banish us – you know!
>
> How dreary – to be – Somebody!
> How public – like a Frog –
> To tell your name – the livelong June –
> To an admiring Bog!
>
> Emily Dickinson

Four years have passed since I completed my group-analytic training. Looking back today, trying to remember how it was, is an exercise fraught with errors. Still, I think this poem gives an impression of how I felt as a group analyst on the first day of the course.

I see it as an important task to try to remember how I felt in those days when I was a trainee. If it is not remembered exactly as it was, that has a meaning too. The experience of what is important tends to change over time.

The five years of training were the most important learning experience in my life, and that was due to the interplay between the different parts of the course and the integrating influence they had on me – all of which made me grow, both professionally and personally.

To write about supervision on the course is to examine in isolation one part, which mainly gets its meaning through the interaction with the other parts. I think that this is a parallel to the relationship between the individual and the group: the individual has a meaning of his or her own, but that meaning is discovered through the interaction with the other members.

What I remember best is the very first intervention directed to me by the supervisor when I first presented a group. I had presented a serious story told by a young woman in the group. I told about the impression it had made on me and the group, and about my intervention, which was a poem full of emotions – not very helpful. Then the supervisor said: 'I appreciate your beautiful way of intervening, using poems and metaphors, and I often use that myself, but I think we should have a look at what is actually happening here. She has told a story about how desperate she feels, she has no job, she has a conflict with her cohabitant which is so serious that she wishes to leave, but she does not know where to go. What would you, the rest of this group, think in this situation?'

Analysing this situation made me realise several important issues:

1 I had to learn to stop dealing with patients in the way I had been trained in individual psychotherapy.
2 I felt taken care of in the situation and safe enough to feel my shame and my limitations. I was at that time in individual psychoanalysis, but I experienced this supervisory session as the starting point of a new kind of journey, my experiential journey to explore my personal psychodynamics in the therapy group and as a conductor.
3 I started to understand the importance of the group process in therapy groups and in the supervision group.
4 When my peers came forward with their reactions to my story in the supervision group, I became aware of the phenomenon of parallel process, and I could understand aspects of the dynamics in my patient group through the emotions brought out in the supervision group.

It is important to state that the impact this supervisory session made on me had to do with the special learning state induced by my emotions in this situation. The supervisor's intervention and the group members' interaction with me made me feel safe enough to come forward and have my thinking and my emotions discussed. I then experienced that when I opened up and gave out something of my inner world I got a lot more back. I realised that when you can experience your emotions and share them with the group, then you are able to use the supervisory group members' associations as possible alternatives for dealing with the material. I understood that supervision is about learning alternatives (or a range of different options) for dealing with group situations.

Later on, I had plenty of time to explore repeatedly my shortcomings. This took place in the here-and-now of the supervisory sessions. I sometimes experienced difficulties there in learning how to change my way of conducting patient groups. The roots of my problems were of two different kinds, which I call my 'dumb spots' and my 'blind spots' (Szecsody 1990).

My 'dumb spots' were when I lacked knowledge and experience, and had to learn the hard way of trial and error, being supervised and reading theory. I am especially grateful to our supervisor for his way of organising the material we brought for supervision. Out of a story which seemed chaotic and disintegrated, he managed to find a focus, to put forward a meaningful question, to raise an intelligent problem for discussion. Gradually we learned how to ask the important questions ourselves, and towards the end of the fifth year we were able to handle them in a 'good-enough' manner. I was sometimes frustrated by the block format of the course. It was not easy to follow a process over time, step by step, meeting only five times a year for two or three days. In our peer-group, I certainly missed a more experienced supervisor, since in our group we were simply peers.

Concerning my 'blind spots', the situation was sometimes more complicated. When I now and again understood that I had difficulties handling a certain topic, it became hard work, often evoking feelings of guilt and shame. I had to make use of my therapy group on the course, and sometimes I could use the large group as a healing ground. The topic was also dealt with in supervision.

Even though I dealt with my personal problems and hang-ups in the small group, as well as in the supervision and the large group, I still needed my individual therapy between the block weekends.

I often wondered: Many of my fellow participants are neither in individual therapy (like me), nor have they been in therapy before starting on this course. How are they then able to integrate all this material? Their difficulties became apparent in different settings (as mine became visible to others). However, being in the same boat gave us a strong feeling of being members of a crew; we all looked forward to the weekends, and came there increasingly eager to present material.

Presenting material in the supervisory sessions became the best way of really getting anything out of the course. Supervision was often the starting point of a trail which led to an awareness of truly emotionally affecting issues, which energised the interactions between us.

So we gradually learned about ourselves and about each other. In the supervisory sessions we learned that we each had our individual ways of thinking, working and defending ourselves in the groups which we conducted. Often these were the very issues we were working through in our small groups. I realised that my learning problems in the supervision were connected with my other problems of interacting therapeutically with patients, and that these again could be handled by the combination of personal therapy and training.

I became increasingly aware that there were no clear boundaries between what I have called 'dumb spots' and 'blind spots', but that there was an important interplay between them. Through the supervision I understood the importance of the working frame which is able to contain the content and the process. I began to look at myself both as a facilitator of the group process and as a part of it. I saw the parallel process in the supervision group and in my patient groups: the conductor's role is one of boundary maintenance, which means that the conductor/supervisor keeps to the primary task and facilitates interaction while moving the group towards fulfilment of the group's goals.

Gradually, I think that my neurotic superego, concerned with 'right' and 'wrong' techniques, theory and results, was softened by the beauty that I saw in the group-analytic experience itself. I became more satisfied with being part of that process in the role as conductor.

When the training came to an end, I felt a bit lonely and depressed, although I had worked through the idealisation and other aspects of my relationships to the teachers. I became afraid that I would not be able to change any more, and that my creativity would be lost.

Then I realised that I had not worked through my relationship to theory, and what theory had meant to me in the process throughout the years of my training. When one goes to a weekend course, one has read some specific theory, and that theory tends to dominate one's thinking for that weekend. This propensity for letting the specific theory for that weekend become too influential, when considering the presented material, had puzzled me. Other points of view tend to be eclipsed by the current theoretical concepts being examined. This, I had thought, had both advantages and disadvantages, but the process would balance itself out in the course of time.

As the end of the Qualifying Course drew near, I established a new, loving relationship with theory, which I have named for myself 'my dialogue with theory'. This is a relationship which I feel to be meaningful; it provides me with affirmation, with opposition, makes me feel guilty and a bit ashamed sometimes, but it is a very healthy relationship, I would contend. Immersion in theory is invigorating; I get a lot of creative ideas, which I like to share with my colleagues. At the same time, it is a reminder of my past, and a pointer towards the future.

REFERENCE – PART II

Szecsody, I. (1990) 'The learning process in psychotherapy supervision' (monograph), Department of Psychiatry, Karolinska Institutet, Stockholm.

Part III A supervisee looks back

Felix Schwarzenbach

I am looking back at five years of training at the *Seminar für Gruppen-analyse*, Zurich. I have learnt a lot from my personal group therapy, the theory sessions, and the supervision, but I have yet to find out whether there is a secret which some group analysts have and some have not, or whether there is no secret, only choosing suitable patients, putting them correctly together into a group, creating and guarding the setting, containing and holding emotions and fantasies, and facilitating interaction: no secret, only skills to be learned, and hard work!

One thing I have learnt which is of great help and affords great relief: to trust the power of the matrix, 'because the health of the group lies in the group'. I participated in the supervision of my group work during the three blocks a year, and I attended continuous supervision between the blocks, since this was required for qualification. The dual supervision helped me to compare and evaluate block and continuous supervision.

One supervision session in the block training which stands out clearly in my mind was marked by a demonstration of everyone in the group, including the supervisor, seemingly losing their minds!

A group was presented with the question why there should have been a marked increase in resistance in an on-going group conducted in a hospital. The group members were suddenly behaving as if they were shoppers in a supermarket – they came and went, missed sessions, came late or left before the end of the session. During the presentation of this group, the supervision group became increasingly agitated and unruly. People talked across each other and seemed not to listen to one another. The supervisor also appeared to be involved in the general confusion, in that she allowed the presentation to overrun its allotted time, thus encroaching on the time of the next presentation. At that moment the supervision group realised that it was behaving differently from its usual manner, probably mirroring the presented group. Had there, too, been a lapse of the usually strictly observed time boundary? It emerged that this had indeed been the case. Due to pressure from the group, the group conductor had allowed the previously observed time of 90 minutes to be extended. Following a discussion of this attack on the setting which had not featured in the presentation, the supervision group once more settled down to its cohesive mode of functioning.

I have learnt from this case that the group presented in supervision in block training is mirrored very accurately and intensely in block supervision. If the supervision group and the supervisor are alert to the intensity of the mirror reaction, the dynamic processes in the group presented emerge very clearly. But the impact is of such intensity that there is a danger of temporarily 'losing one's mind' in the supervision group – and this is a novel and disconcerting experience for me.

> A group with psychiatric outpatients, all of whom were on medication (lithium), was presented in a supervision block. The atmosphere in this group had been receptive, caring and holding. The talk was about the experience of the medication and the treatment received. The verbal exchanges were open and constructive. The group conductor, a psychiatrist, had knowledge of something the other group members had not – namely, that he had been offered an interesting position in another town. He had so far not informed the group of his planned departure, because, he said, contracts had not yet been exchanged. In the next session, the atmosphere in the group underwent a subtle change, culminating in an aggressive dispute about immigrants, refugees and Second World War experiences. During the presentation of the group in supervision a few weeks later, it became clear to the presenter that the group had sensed his imminent departure, which they had experienced as destruction and desertion. The supervision group wondered whether the information of his imminent departure had been withheld from the group because the group conductor had felt guilt over his desertion of the group to further his own professional needs and wishes. He now understood the group's reaction of anger, aggression and fear, and this enabled him and the group to work towards, and finally experience, the grief involved in the loss.

The emotional responses to new members joining and old members leaving become very clear and meaningful when presented to the supervision group in block training, since they are mirrored by the slow-open experiential groups of the training course, where the impact of arrival, departure and separation are yearly occurrences. The experience and the working-through of these universal and crucial themes constitute one of the strong points of block training in group analysis.

Some of the obvious drawbacks come readily to mind. For one, the presentation of one's group cannot be detailed. Questions of technique and strategy can usually only be touched on but seldom studied and followed up. The supervision session often comes long after the reported events have taken place, the proposed responses no longer fit the on-going group processes, and an important opportunity for an appropriate intervention may be missed. Feedback from the supervision group and the supervisor are delayed and corrections which utilise the insights and emotional responses that the trainee conductor takes from supervision cannot be applied in the appropriate sessions. There is therefore less support for the trainee conductor's immediate work. There is also less emotional support, since intimacy and warmth generated and held in a supervision group which meets so infrequently cannot match that of an on-going supervision group. Usually members of the supervision group are less well-informed about the supervisees' professional working situations. All this gives less encouragement to the new trainee in starting to work as a group psychotherapist and to find an identity in this new therapeutic field of activity.

When I consider all these experiences in my training as a group analyst, it becomes clear to me that the question of continuous training versus block training is not a straight choice, not a true alternative; ideally I would want to have both. Block supervision has advantages which are due to its unique setting as, for example, the long intervals between blocks. These allow for a more objective, process-oriented view on the conducting of the group. The drawbacks, such as the delay in the feedback between the presented processes and their supervision, are hard to overcome. Thus to satisfy the needs of a professional training there should be provision made in the block training for an accompanying continuous supervision, possibly with the help of a regular group telephone interchange, or through regular peer supervision between blocks. It is clear to me that block and continuous supervision are complementary rather than mutually exclusive. I would not want to miss the chance to have both.

Chapter 10

Supervision on the Manchester block course

Stephen Cogill

Until 1989, training as a group analyst in the United Kingdom was available only in London, and access to training was limited to those within reach of the metropolis. In 1989 a new course of training was established in Manchester to open up training to candidates from any part of the UK. This was achieved by adopting a 'block' structure based upon training schemes established in many European countries.

The main elements of training are contained within a three-day weekend 'block': group-analytic therapy, theoretical seminars, and clinical supervision. A very significant feature of block training is the inclusion of large group sessions as an opportunity for integration of the training experience in the context of the entire training community, permitting exploration of developing professional identity, and of changing relations with staff and other students, as a member of the training course as an 'institution'. Ten such blocks take place each year.

Within the block format, supervision and the trainee's group-analytic psychotherapy are in very close juxtaposition. The trainee has the opportunity to take up in the therapeutic group any puzzling, perplexing, or extreme responses encountered in supervision. This interchange is eased in the block format by all members of the therapeutic group being in training. The predicament of the training therapist is therefore deeply understood in the therapeutic group. 'Professional' defences are therefore frequently subject to analysis and modification in the therapy of trainees, sometimes fuelled by 'data' from the supervision context.

Course members are drawn from throughout the UK. Although a few work in departments of psychotherapy quite as sophisticated as any in London, many course members work in settings where psychotherapeutic principles are less fully understood and accepted. Not a few course members have had to deal with corrosive scepticism or the outright hostility of colleagues and managers. This has had several implications. Many trainees have felt the need for the companionship and support provided by supervision far more frequently than once each month or five weeks. Much early work in supervision has been devoted to the creation of a setting in which group-analytic therapy can be carried out. This has involved attention to network building, to negotiations with management and with colleagues, and to the 'missionary' role of the group analyst.

PEER GROUPS MARK I

It quickly became clear, as course members began to assemble their training groups, that supervision each month or six weeks would not be sufficient to allay their anxieties as novice group therapists, nor to provide opportunities for trouble-shooting unexpected developments threatening the students' training groups. These sometimes amounted to clinical emergencies. While overseas courses meeting less frequently than ten times each year invariably include dual supervision, with course supervision augmented by local supervision arrangements, in Manchester many trainees were obliged to rely exclusively upon supervision provided as part of the training course. This was particularly so for trainees coming from the more far-flung regions of the UK.

A network of 'peer groups' was therefore developed in consultation with the students. Composition was dictated primarily by geographic considerations, although from the outset peer groups had to contain members from more than one therapeutic group, in order to minimise boundary problems. Inevitably, peer groups varied in the demands they made of course members. Some had to travel long distances to participate in peer group meetings. Others were more fortunate. Naturally, some peer groups were perceived as more attractive than others. The venue for the peer group meeting in some cases was bitterly contested. Although the additional supervision provided by the peer group was generally appreciated, nonetheless the peer group became a focus for anti-task processes within the training institution. Bearing in mind that the peer group, alone among the various meetings and events of the training, took place outside the confines of the block weekends, it is scarcely surprising that anti-task forces should there find a rallying point.

All manner of interpersonal differences, rivalries, and unexpressed resentments at the demands of training condensed in the peer group, creating elements of an anti-task group culture.

Although peer groups were constructed so that not all members would come from the same therapeutic group, it was impossible to avoid some members of the same therapeutic group being brought together in a peer group. Although 'chaperoned' by peer group members from other therapy groups, it was noticeable that when interpersonal difficulties occurred in the peer group, they were frequently between members of the same therapeutic group. Fortunately, the peer group members quickly learned where to take the different kinds of problems: to the small group, to the large group, or 'to the coffee break'!

Many of the rivalries and other interpersonal difficulties revealed by the peer group experience were taken by supervisees to be analysed in the small group so that more effective use could be made of the peer group supervision. Other problems required the attention of the large group. From the beginning, differences of North and South, of rich and poor, had occupied the large group. This was inevitable in a training course taking place in the underprivileged North of England, and staffed by group analysts from London! At this stage rumour began to circulate within the training community about the relative merits of the different peer groups. It had a familiar ring: the peer groups appeared to belong to the two great families, the 'haves' and the 'have-nots'. This rich vein was mined in the large group.

Another polarisation was that between the peer group and the weekend block supervision group. Naturally, early in their training, members of the course were comparatively inexperienced, and it was inevitable that the peer group should be felt to be less valuable and resourceful than the weekend block supervision which included an experienced group analyst supervisor. This difference was sometimes amplified distinctly in the minds of trainees whose own low self-esteem and self-denigration, combined with the projection onto supervisors of exaggerated skills and knowledge, created a dynamic in which the peer group was devalued. In the view of the supervisors, considerable clinical acumen and group-analytic grasp was to be found in the peer groups, but many trainees were unable yet to trust their colleagues and themselves and struggled to rely excessively on weekend block supervision, and on the London supervisor.

Block training has many of the features of a therapeutic community. Peer group supervision, as initially organised in the Diploma training, took place beyond the boundary of the training community. In a training course otherwise strongly structured, peer group supervision represented the unknown in the equation. It is tempting to understand the initial difficulties encountered in peer group supervision as an epidemic of 'acting out' in response to boundary weakness. Considerable thought was given to this first year's experience of peer group supervision, and course members were consulted about what improvements should be made.

PEER GROUPS MARK II

Expansion of the training course and of the number of supervisors after eighteen months permitted peer group and weekend block supervision group to be brought together as a single supervision group. From this point in the training, supervision was from a single group, although only including the group analyst supervisor during weekend blocks. This development had several advantages. When peer group and weekend block supervision had been separate, a report had been provided by the peer group on their meeting, but it had not always proved possible for supervisors to monitor the 'process' of the peer group effectively. Once peer group and weekend block groups were brought together, the supervisor was far more easily able to keep in touch with the process of the supervision group while meeting as a peer group. The polarisation between peer group and weekend group virtually disappeared, and the course members' perception of supervision received from the peer group appeared to climb dramatically. The developing confidence of course members as group-analytic psychotherapists was on the whole sustained in peer group sessions. A more containing supervision structure appears to have been created which has enabled supervision groups to keep to 'task' far more fully and successfully.

FURTHER DEVELOPMENTS

Several course members living in more outlying parts of the UK were unable to travel regularly to peer group sessions. It was therefore decided to experiment with the use of 'telephone conference' facilities as an alternative to the face-to-face peer groups. A telephone conference is an arrangement whereby a number of people are put in telephone contact with each other via a private line. The procedure is straight-forward although advance booking is needed. As telephone conferences are expensive, it was necessary to limit the session to sixty minutes, a much shorter time than would be devoted to a peer group session. The great advantage is the inclusion of the supervisor, even if based hundreds of miles away.

Telephone conference supervision has been found to be surprisingly effective. Although, prior to the trial, considerable concern was expressed regarding the depth of communication that would be achieved over the telephone, it has been found that when supervisees and supervisor have worked together face-to-face and know each other's groups, very effective and economical communication can be achieved. The supervision process is altered in certain respects. The supervisee has to arrive at a clear focus for his or her brief presentation. The emphasis has been more strongly upon the responses of the supervisor than on the contributions of other supervisees or on the 'process' of the supervision group. Many presentations have had a problem-solving focus. Naturally the time boundary must be managed carefully and precisely in telephone conference supervision. Supervisors report playing a more active structuring and facilitating role during the telephone conference supervision to ensure that supervision material is quickly brought into sharp focus.

Bringing together peer group and weekend block supervision greatly improved consistency, continuity, and containment in supervision. Telephone conference supervision has taken this process a stage further, and is generally regarded as a surprisingly successful medium for supervision. It is therefore planned to extend telephone conference arrangements to all supervision groups in the Diploma training course. It has not yet been decided whether this should augment or replace peer group supervision. One spin-off from peer group meetings had been the development of a local network where sometimes none has previously existed. Extension of training from three to four years in 1992 permitted a further development. While supervision continued for only three years, trainees often felt under some pressure to start their training groups as early as possible. Four years' supervision allows scope for an initial supervision group for all those in the first year of training.

Trainees in a block training programme have their group analysis in a group in which all members are trainees. The time structure is also radically different from that of a 'continuous' twice-weekly group. Trainees do not therefore necessarily see their group analyst, and their group, dealing with such matters as lateness, absence, etc. Block trainees therefore require particular attention to basic questions of dynamic administration early in their supervision period. Developing and maintaining a professional network, preparing the setting (physical, social, and organisational), selection and composition of the group, and 'boundary management' receive particular emphasis which will be repaid when fewer teething troubles are encountered in early sessions of trainees' groups. The first year supervision group provides scope for 'coaching' in the skills of dynamic administration, while preparatory work is going on towards forming the training group after the first year of seminars. This arrangement has the added advantage that trainees who need a longer period in therapy prior to conducting the training group can more easily defer starting until they are ready.

OVERVIEW

There are many differences between the once-weekly group conducted under supervision by a trainee and the experience of being in a twice-weekly group for group analysis, for students in continuous training. For students in block training, the experience of group analysis as therapy organised in blocks differs still further from their own supervised group conducting. It is not surprising therefore that block trainees experience greater initial difficulty in dynamic administration than do trainees undergoing continuous training. On the other hand, many block trainees become particularly adept in this crucial aspect of the group analyst's role, and it is interesting to note that a majority of clinical papers presented by Diploma candidates deal with themes of dynamic administration.

Chapter 11

A Greek model of supervision

The matrix as supervisor – a version of peer supervision developed at IGA (Athens)

Yannis K. Tsegos

> Just as the patient communicates to the therapist how he needs to be treated,
> so the group becomes a good supervisor of the therapist who wants to learn.
> (Grotjahn 1987: 129)

INTRODUCTION

Supervision, according to the *Oxford English Dictionary*, is 'looking or viewing from above', thus defining the act of supervision as a unilateral one. In therapeutic, and more specifically in psychotherapeutic practice, the supervision process takes place when a senior or experienced trainer looks at the psychotherapeutic work of the apprentice, whose task is to learn how to treat another individual. Regarding the relationship between the two (i.e. supervisor–supervisee) this bears many psycho-dynamic features, resembling the situation between therapist and patient, creating a lot of transferential feelings, and it is also coloured by the constant 'presence' of the absent third party (i.e. the patient). In other words we have here a kind of a group of three, where the third person, the patient, although absent, influences the relationship of the other two intensely, and of course decisively. As for the transferential/counter-transferential vicissitudes of this dyadic relationship, these have been extensively discussed in psychoanalytic literature, and the tradi-tional remedy for those difficulties is usually more analysis for the supervisee, but very rarely or never for the supervisor.

This same type of supervision, i.e. the dyadic, is followed even in some group psychotherapy training institutions, and is conducted on a one-to-one-basis, following the traditional psychoanalytic model. There is no doubt that this method contrasts sharply with the basic group-analytic approach, which, as regards therapy in particular, is based on the full participation of all relevant participants, i.e. the group, and not

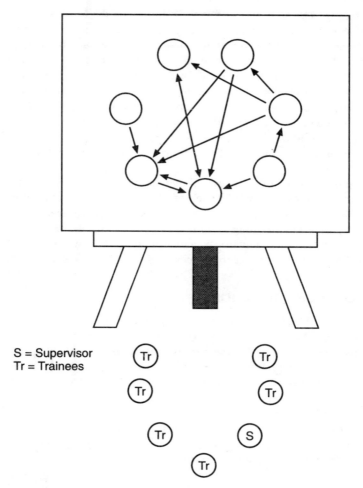

Figure 11.1 Supervision in the classical way

so much on the knowledge of the expert (conductor). We may underline here that the psychoanalytic way of therapy, as well as supervision, treats the patient or the trainee either as an object or as an individual. Group analysis approaches both of them as *persons*. I think the difference is cardinal.

Fortunately, in most training institutions, and in particular at the Institute of Group Analysis in London, supervision takes place in a group setting. The students present their groups on the blackboard in front of an experienced supervisor and a group of fellow students. There is no doubt that the presence and participation of the group contributes a lot towards fostering a more horizontal dialogue and restrains, to some extent, vertical communication, intellectualisation, etc. (see Figure 11.1).

The 'third party' participates through the account brought by the trainee. In group supervision the presented group is again absent, but 'present' through the account of the trainee. Nevertheless here too there is in fact a *real* third party present, the group of fellow students; these may at times act as an ally or advocate or even as an opponent of the absent group.

In summary, in the classical group-analytic type of supervision, and in contrast to the psychoanalytic one, the situation is multi-factorial: it is comprised of the supervisee, the supervisor, the student's account of his or her group, and the group of the other trainees. What we have here, of course, is a complicated multi-dynamic situation which we are called upon either to 'tame' or to accept as such, and to make the most of.

GENERAL CONSIDERATIONS

Supervision constitutes a decisive part of learning in any kind of training. Without getting into details of the theory of learning we may single out, somewhat arbitrarily for the purposes of the present chapter, the factors of Knowledge Information, in order to examine them more closely. Information can be acquired more easily by the interested person in a variety of ways (e.g. reading, listening to lectures, tapes, etc.) but it is short-lived, of limited use, devoid of experience, and is usually reserved for unsophisticated matters. As for knowledge, this is more rich, more complex as it presupposes a certain degree of unlearning, it relates to the object but mainly concerns the subject who is pursuing it; it is acquired mainly by means of experience, which is influenced greatly by interaction with others, preferably more than one, and by the setting, which has to be appropriate to the task.

The matter of concern here is to teach students group psychotherapy. In other words to teach them to act appropriately in groups following the group-analytic approach. The student therefore has to learn how to act as a facilitator instead of interpreting, to learn how to promote horizontal relationships and free-floating discussion, while at the same time avoiding monologue, etc.

Students in group-analytic institutes are mainly influenced by three types of experience: by participating in their own personal therapy groups, by conducting their own therapy group and by the supervision procedure. In supervision, regardless of the teacher's attitudes, the manner of teaching is greatly influenced by the setting, and there is no doubt that in the group world the trainee needs to be protected from the didactic type of teaching, which may result in reinforcing the roles of expert–novice.

The classical group setting in supervision (i.e. IGA London and others) contains a lot of positive elements conducive to creating a suitable and knowledge-enhancing experience, such as the presence of a group of fellow students conducted by an experienced group analyst. This setting can minimise inhibitions stemming from super-egotistical situations which may occur as a result of the presence of an experienced conductor or even of fellow students who may play this role for a while. However, supervision carries the burden of an authoritarian tradition, and in conjunction with the anxiety of the inexperienced and regressed trainee, the supervisory process may be transformed into an authoritarian relationship, even if this takes place in the presence of third persons, i.e. students, and even if the supervisor is brought up in the group-analytic tradition. But certainly, following Abercrombie (1983), our aim is not to establish authoritarian attitudes, but rather to encourage all students to become authorities in their own right.

The title of this volume is aptly *The Third Eye*. This introduces the concept already discussed, but as this may mean several things, I think we need to consider the nature of this third 'eye'. Is it the eye of the expert, which the student is definitely very much in need of, or are we referring to something deeper and more enriched which emerges from the *matrix* of the supervision session comprising the interaction of different persons and factors, such as fellow students, the presenting student, the account of the presented group session, the experienced senior colleague (conductor) and the interrelations in this network? There is no doubt that the presence of this matrix is very strong and influential. The question is how to make use of it without disturbing it.

The classical method was used initially in the group-analytic training course in Athens for about three years (1979–1981). These were the years when the present author was trying to set up an open day clinic and at the same time to introduce group analysis in Greece, following the guidelines of the Institute of Group Analysis (London) where I had been trained. As regards supervision, I had of course been taught in the classical method in London, my supervisor being Malcolm Pines. During these very valuable years in London, supervision was one of the most important parts of the training; I remember very clearly our supervision sessions in the afternoon in Bickenhall Mansions with Malcolm interfering very rarely, with an active and creative participation on the students' part, as he allowed the group to take full responsibility for the work, to the extent that he sometimes gave the impression of falling asleep!

It was natural that later, when I was myself a supervisor, I had this model very vividly in my mind, trying to get into my supervisor's shoes! But as I was comparing the two pictures I found my own image lacking considerably by comparison. I was not confident at all, not happy, and the group definitely was quite anxious and not very productive. In that situation I could not possibly pretend to fall asleep! I was of course aware that I was a different person with no experience, but even that was not a great comfort to me. Neither was the realisation that under the circumstances of that period, I had also to act as therapist to my students (to three out of the four), and as supervisor, theoretical seminar leader and colleague in the context of the day clinic.

With such unhappy feelings, thoughts and doubts during these very valuable, very turbulent and creative years, the training of the first generation of group analysts in Greece, consisting of four persons, was completed. Or was it? By the end of 1981 I had to decide if I was going to qualify them as group analysts, which I wanted very much to do. But I was not sure if my affirmative decision was based so much on the quality of their training, or on their own qualities as persons, or even my own pressure to set up the Institute. However, I decided to put my apprehensions aside and to qualify them, and it was with them that we founded the Institute in Athens, in December 1982.[1]

A NEW APPROACH: WHEN NECESSITY BECOMES A VIRTUE

In the meantime, new groups of trainees started and there was more work to be done, but now it was possible to delegate some of my own responsibilities to my new colleagues, starting with the theoretical seminars. This was a great relief and I had started to feel more relaxed and was able to make a number of observations regarding supervision. The first observation was of course the considerable anxiety which occurred, leading at times to unwillingness to present a group session, particularly among the more inexperienced students, in spite of the supervisor's encouragement and support. This anxiety was clearly connected with the fear of being criticised by the supervisor or by their own fellow students. In addition there was a tendency for the supervised students to say the 'right thing', anticipating the preference of the supervisor. There was similarly a tendency to imitate the style of the conductor of their personal therapy group when conducting their own group, and an inclination on the student-presenter's part to 'improve', shape, or even falsify or 'forget' material in order to avoid criticism.

A gross discrepancy between the actual session and the presented one was confirmed by comparing the therapist and the co-therapist accounts which were written separately for the same session (Kakouri and Tsegos 1993). We also observed that fellow-students tended to make comments or criticism according to the preference of the supervisor, and they tended occasionally to show off newly acquired knowledge, in the theoretical seminars, occasionally somewhat crudely. In addition, the usual competitive phenomena among students tended to inhibit and block the supervisory process.

Probably as a result of all these factors, there was a marked tendency for intellectualisation, theoretical discussions and a noticeable dependency on the supervisor. The whole process took place in a very anxious atmosphere for both the trainees and the supervisor, and supervision was definitely not one of the most popular activities of the training! However, during that time it often happened that I let the trainees run some of their theoretical seminars on their own due to my own overloaded schedule. To my relief, during my absence, not only did things not get out of hand, they got better. After that, I deliberately let them do the supervision sometimes on their own (without my presence). However, I was given the signal that I could not do this too often. I discussed my thoughts and anxieties with my first students and later on with new ones, in one of the sensitivity meetings that we had established. Although they agreed with some of my observations, they nevertheless saw the situation as something normal or expected. It seemed that only I was unhappy, therefore I tried to find a possible new technique, more suitable for an inexperienced supervisor. I experimented with different settings and processes until one morning in February 1983, I was struck with the idea that instead of commenting on the account presented already on the blackboard, I could ask my students to express their own feelings and fantasies. It seems that this request did the trick, as the whole atmosphere changed completely and the comments on the presented group became more accurate and, what's more, they were to a large extent related to the feelings and fantasies expressed before. It is beyond the purpose of this chapter to describe the experimentation that took place in the following months, which eventually led to a process divided into three stages: the Presentation, the Analysis and the Synthesis (Figure 11.2A).

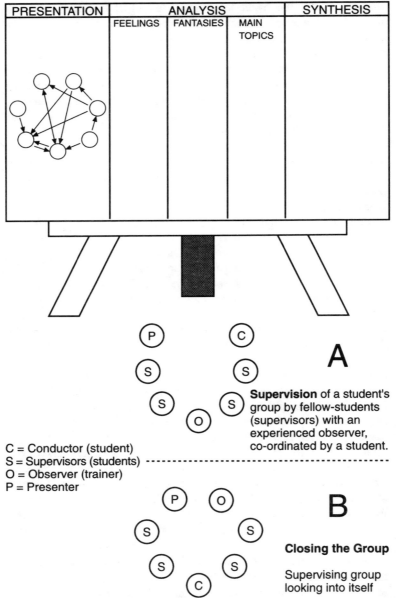

C = Conductor (student)
S = Supervisors (students)
O = Observer (trainer)
P = Presenter

A

Supervision of a student's group by fellow-students (supervisors) with an experienced observer, co-ordinated by a student.

B

Closing the Group

Supervising group looking into itself

Figure 11.2 Two phases of peer supervision

During the Presentation stage, a group is presented in the usual way with the student reading out his or her notes and marking group exchanges on the blackboard.

It is agreed that supervision is now undertaken by the whole group (supervising group) which is a group in its own right, with a fixed time and place of meeting, conducted by one of the students, while a 'trainer' (or supervisor in the old sense) is present only as an experienced observer.

The supervising group sits in a semi-circle in front of the blackboard and is expected to take an active part in the second stage of supervision. This is the Analysis, which follows the Presentation stage. During the Analysis each of the 'supervisor-students' follows the presentation procedure and records in a special format (the Supervision Protocol, see below) the following:

- His or her feelings during or after the presentation;
- His or her fantasies (images that passed through the mind during the presentation);
- What are perceived as the main themes or topics of the presented group.

After the presentation, when all the students have written down their fantasies, feelings and main topics, the conductor-student asks each of the others to read out their notes and then writes these out on the blackboard.

The final stage is the Synthesis of all this material, in which the whole group takes part, including the experienced observer, and they try to connect the material presented with that produced in the supervising group as now seen on the blackboard. After all this, there may be some suggestions concerning the technique or the way that the therapist or therapists made their interpretations.

At times the supervising group gives evidence that it is blocked, or that it is not productive, or that there is something 'going on' in relation to the material offered by the supervising group during the Analysis stage. Such occurrences usually arise as a repercussion of mirroring or resonance phenomena coming from the presented group, or indeed because something is 'going on' in the supervising group.

If this is not noticed by the supervising group, or if it is avoided or denied, then, and only then, is it time for the experienced observer to ask if there is something missing or 'going on' and to suggest that there may be a need for the group to 'close the circle' and look at itself (Figure 11.2B). In this case the presenting student sits down, the circle is closed and the whole group is involved in a 'here-and-now' situation.

Supervision Protocol
1. Supervisory session of the ... year students
2. Present no.: ....   3. Absent (names): ....
4. Name ....

PRESENTATION

Presented Group

5. Type of Group
   Group analytic ☐
   Experiential ☐
   Sociotherapeutic ☐
   Psychodrama ☐
6. Therapist
   (Presenter) ....
   Co-therapist
   (Presenter) ....
7. Date of session ....
8. Location ....
9. Time ....
10. Frequency ....
11. Absences ....

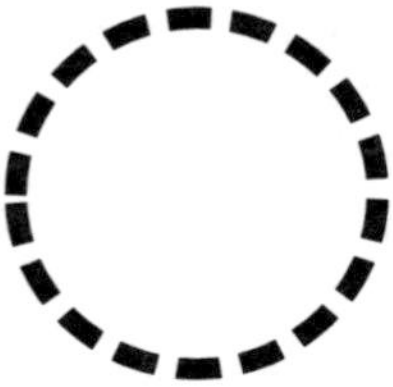

12.

Supervisory Group

13. Conductor (student)...
14. Observer (trainer).......
15. Location ....
16. Date ....
17. Time ....

18. Additional Information

ANALYSIS

19. Feelings	20. Fantasies	21. Themes – Topics

SYNTHESIS

22. Comments and Conclusions

23. Was there a need to 'close the circle'?   YES ☐ NO ☐

24. Who intervened?   Conductor ☐ Observer ☐ Supervisor-students ☐

Figure 11.3 Supervision Protocol

The whole procedure can be clarified further by examining the Supervision Protocol itself (Fig. 11.3).

THE SUPERVISION PROTOCOL

Initially the instructions for the new procedure were verbal. Later on, there was a simple paper with some crude instructions. Finally it became evident that a clearly defined structure was not only necessary, but was one of the most important parts of this method.

The Supervision Protocol (SP), which was a result of that realisation, not only makes the role of the conductor – who is a student – easier, but structures the whole process itself. The version currently in use serves as a rule of thumb even to very inexperienced students, enabling them to participate in the supervisory procedure right from the beginning actively and effectively. The SP sheets are distributed by the conductor-student to each of the students in the group and to the observer. The completed SPs are kept by the students throughout their own training and handed over at the end of the training along with the notes of their own group. (They represent part of the clinical requirements for matriculation.)

The various parts of the SP provide important information for dynamic (structural) and practical, as well as research purposes. Each heading is explained below:

1 The year or class of the supervisory group (e.g. 3rd, 4th year, etc.), regardless of the study year of the therapist-presenter. The therapist may, if under pressure or for other reasons, go to another year's supervisory group.
2 The number of students present in the supervisory group, including the observer (trainer).
3 Names of absentees (student or observer).
4 Name of the person filling out the SP sheet (student or observer).

Presentation

Under this heading is included material concerning the presented group, the blackboard, the supervisory group, and any additional information.

5 Defines the type of presented group. Besides proper group-analytic groups, students also present the experiential groups of the Introductory Course, because it is part of their training to participate in it and to become conductors or co-conductors of such groups. As this method of supervision has also been adopted by the Training

Course organised by the Open Psychotherapeutic Centre for Socio-therapists (Therapeutic Community staff) and Psychodramatists, the SP also allows for Sociotherapeutic and Psychodrama groups.

6   Name of the therapist or the co-therapist.
7   Date of the session.
8   Location of the group (private practice, day centre, hospital, etc.).
9   Time the group takes place (e.g. 7.30–9.00 p.m.).
10 Frequency of the group (once weekly, once a fortnight, etc.).
11 Names of members absent from group.

The supervisory group covers:

12 A miniature copy of the blackboard is provided so that the student can copy the group as presented on the real blackboard.
13 Name of the conductor-student of the supervisory group.
14 Name of the experienced observer (trainer).
15 Location of the supervision session. It usually takes place in the premises of the Institute, but it is important to know if there has been a change, for dynamic reasons.
16 Date of supervision session.
17 Time the supervisory group takes place. The frequency is not noted as it is known that supervisory groups take place on a once-weekly basis. The duration is two hours and sometimes it can be extended.
18 Under 'additional information', space is provided for any further notes.

Analysis

This heading includes material which emerges as a result of the presentation. The supervisors, as well as the observer, obviously get a lot of feelings, fantasies, as well as concrete material such as themes and topics from the presentation.

19 'Feelings': a supervising student may, for example, experience feelings of emptiness, euphoria, sadness, fear, expectation, anger, etc., which would be recorded here.
20 'Fantasies' – or free associations, e.g. the feeling of being at the bottom of a well, or being on a cruise boat, or having lunch with friends, or making plans about future holidays, etc.

(Both feelings and fantasies are encouraged to be as free as possible, without any censorship, regardless of their relevance to the material being presented.)

21 'Themes and topics' – the supervising students or the observer record here certain events of the presented group, such as particular behaviour of the patients and therapists, a specific intervention which made an impression on them, as well as their impression as to the main theme of the session of the presented group.

(The recording of the above three main parts of the Analysis on paper is intended to discourage the student from being influenced by what others say.)

All this is read aloud and recorded by the presenting therapist on the blackboard, next to the drawing of the group. A convention has been adopted whereby each column is written in a different colour: feelings are written in yellow, fantasies in red and themes in blue.

Synthesis

After all the material of the Analysis stage has been recorded on the blackboard, there follows a discussion chaired by the 'conductor-student' concerning the interrelation of all the material produced, representing the repercussions of the presented session.

22 If there is evidence that the material produced in 'feelings', 'fantasies' and 'topics' makes sense, the session is completed with relief.

23 On the other hand, if there is a lot of irrelevance and incoherence, followed by a tense atmosphere, the group tries to find the reason for this; it may be a repercussion of something relevant to the presented material; if not, there is a need for the observing group to look at itself. In this case someone from the group intervenes and suggests the group should 'close' the semi-circle to form a circle, in which the therapist-presenter is included. A proper group session then takes place and the group contemplates the question 'What is going on among us here and now?' At this stage the role of the observer is important, for he or she may be the only one to see what actually is going on in the present group, and may intervene in order to suggest the closing of the group. This is where there is a resistance to accept that there is something 'going on' in the present group which is mirrored in the clinical material, and this is the reason for recording specifically:

24 Who intervened in order to close the circle.

CONCLUDING REMARKS

This model has been used quite extensively for ten years in supervising several kinds of groups, i.e. group-analytic, sociotherapeutic, psychodramatic, family groups, both within the context of the Open Psychotherapeutic Centre of Athens, the Institute of Group Analysis (Athens), and also experimentally in some institutes in Europe. It appears to contribute a lot towards creating a relaxed atmosphere and reduces the hesitation of inexperienced students to present their own group. It also seems to contribute to the trainee's personal development by promoting self-confidence, flexibility and creative adult thinking and prevents unnecessary regression and dependency. It also helps the trainee to differentiate between power and strength (Tsegos 1993), by placing emphasis on the group instead of the conductor. Although a formal research study has not been conducted yet, there is strong evidence that the quality of the therapy sessions is positively influenced.

Besides the above, it is helpful in distinguishing between the dynamic and foundation matrix and it is particularly useful in cotherapy, where it can reveal the dynamics of the partnership and prevent future problems. Its use of a structured and detailed written account of the session enables it to be used also for studying group phenomena, such as mirroring, resonance, etc. (Kouneli *et al.* 1992), and for other research purposes. This model of supervision seems to be the most akin to the group-analytic approach but, as a new method, it can be more productive if the experienced observer is convinced of its usefulness, and the context (institution) in which it takes place trusts the group more than the experts. The personality of the experienced observer and the quality of the supervising group also play a decisive role, particularly at the beginning. Another precondition of the method is the full comprehension of the essence of it, by the observer as well as the trainees, and for this reason during the initial sessions the 'conductor-student' may need to take a more active role. Last but not least, one of the key requirements of the method is that the experienced observer should aspire more towards enjoying his role than exercising it.

I presented this version of supervision in a very crude and primitive form in Zagreb (Tsegos 1984) at which my supervisor was present. At the end of the session he congratulated me and commented that my approach constituted a kind of 'inner releasing vision'. At that time I took it as an encouraging gesture, which was not unusual from him. Now, as ten years have passed, I have fewer doubts that it was said only in encouragement.

NOTE

1 Their names are: Dr Atha Kakouri, Psychiatrist; Mrs Eleni Morarou, PSW; Mr Thalis Papadakis and Mrs Zoe Voyatzaki, Psychologists, now experienced training group analysts, colleagues and friends.

REFERENCES

Abercrombie, M.L.J. (1983) 'The application of some principles of group analytic psychotherapy to higher education', in M. Pines (ed.) *The Evolution of Group Analysis*, London: Routledge & Kegan Paul.

Grotjahn, M. (1987) *My Favourite Patient: The Memoirs of a Psychoanalyst*, Frankfurt: Peter Lang.

Kakouri, A. and Tsegos, I.K. (1993) 'Boundaries and barriers in peer supervision', paper presented at the 9th European Symposium in Group Analysis, Heidelberg, 29 August–4 September.

Kouneli, E., Tsegos, I.K. and Karaolidou, M. (1992) 'The group analytic supervision: the significance of the peer group in the supervision of psychotherapy trainees', paper presented at 4th Panhellenic Conference in Psychology, Athens, 16–19 April.

Tsegos, I.K. (1984) 'Experimenting on group analytic supervision', paper presented at the 6th European Symposium in Group Analysis, Zagreb, 1–3 September.

Tsegos, I.K. (1993) 'Strength, power and group analysis', *Group Analysis* 26: 131–137.

Chapter 12

Effects of institutional dynamics

Victoria Graham Fuller

I will attempt a broad look at supervision within an institutional setting in order to highlight dynamic processes, both between and within its internal structures, or sub-groups. Through exploring issues specific to a particular institution, I will show how trainee, staff and administrative groups reflect each other's concerns and anxieties in unconscious ways, and how this influences the relationships between groups and the individuals who inhabit them.

Anxiety is an established thread in the emotional fabric of any organisation and perhaps can never be dispelled. Conscious attempts to address it, however, and to identify themes shared throughout the organisation, may help to mitigate its disruptive potential. This chapter focuses on one organisation and its methods of coping with inevitable anxiety caused in part by the nature of its work and the issues which arise from it; it attempts to 'freeze frame' a time in the life of the organisation when the procedure for collection and storage of information was under review. Themes common to life in institutions, such as personal exposure, identity, and assessment (or personal worth), all of which may generate anxiety, are considered in the light of how they were expressed in various sub-groups within the organisation.

The institution under consideration is a psychotherapy clinic serving a large artistic community in the midwestern United States; although a small city in its own right, it is close enough to the state capital to be within commuting distance for employees of the federal government offices there.

The aim of the institution is two-fold: to provide therapy to the local community and to offer training placements in the practice of psychotherapy. Trainees receive didactic teaching while carrying out clinical work with clients on a 'constant assessment' basis. Staff and trainees represent a wide range of disciplines within the health care field, including social work, primary medical care, counselling, and psychiatry as well as, to a lesser degree, group and family therapy. Most trainees continue their employment in these fields during placement, which may last up to three or four years. Supervision of trainees takes place weekly in small groups conducted by one senior staff member. Staff supervisors meet regularly to discuss work-related issues, but do not undergo supervision themselves in any formal sense, although some are supervised outside the institution. All trainees attend an experiential group in the institution as part of their training.

At the particular time of this study, two major organisational changes were under way. The administration, in consultation with the staff, was implementing procedural and policy changes made necessary by the installation of new computers to store information from records and client files. The new system was designed to allow clients access to their files which meant that, for the first time, trainees would be required to store summaries of session notes, and they would now be responsible for their own notes rather than keeping them on the premises – another departure from established routine. Simultaneously, one of the groups of staff supervisors was considering the possibility of organising a more formal kind of supervision of trainees' work than they had previously been used to. This was in response to questions within the group about the value of the present method, which was more consultative than supervisory, and about what sort of model was being offered to trainees by supervisors who were not themselves currently undertaking supervision as an integral part of their work in the institution.

THEORY OF INSTITUTIONAL DYNAMICS

In his chapter 'Group Dynamics – A Review', Bion (1961) tells us that when faced with the demands and complexities of group life, adults will resort to coping mechanisms which are typical of infant mental life and which are necessary as primitive defences against overwhelming anxieties. Eliot Jacques showed in his own pioneering work that groups of people who work together develop shared attitudes and beliefs for the purpose of essential psychological defence. Jacques described the way individuals externalise their own internal worlds into the institution of which they are a part through splitting and projective identification. Specific anxieties may be kept at bay through this unconscious method although, he pointed out, there is a price to pay (Jacques, as quoted in Hinshelwood 1987). This will be further explored below.

ANXIETY

In the psychotherapy clinic there was ample justification for collective anxiety. Trainees, who were accustomed to being effective and auto-nomous in their places of work, were placed in a dependent learning situation in which they understandably felt deskilled and infantilised. They were faced, some for the first time, with the task of offering psychotherapy to disturbed clients who exposed them to projections of infantile helplessness and rage which required containment. Further-more, at the end of each placement year, trainees underwent an assess-ment procedure, in consultation with their supervisors, to determine their position in the training. This process created heightened anxiety on the part of trainees and staff alike and induced a shared prevailing fear of exposure in their work.

Supervisors, for their part, routinely supervised the work of up to six trainees at a time, each of whom might bring as many as half a dozen clients into each supervision group: a possible total of thirty-six souls in one room for ninety minutes. Common features of group supervision, for example, feelings of deprivation, rivalry, jealousy and shame among trainees, were highlighted and at times exacerbated by the need to share limited time as well as to be accountable for the quality of their work, all of which placed pressure on supervisors to contain the persecutory anxiety in their groups and hold trainees' projections of a depriving, withholding parental figure.

Trainees were expected, as a cultural norm of the institution, to express their anxiety, arising from their perception of deprivation and 'lack of excellence' in comparison to their fellow trainees, and most supervisors considered it part of their responsibility to help trainees in their groups to be in touch with all responses relevant to their work. Supervisors, on the other hand, seldom spoke directly of their share of the culture's anxiety and frustration, although end-of-term fatigue and occasional eruptions about the strain of dealing with an especially defensive trainee might be shared in the privacy of the staff room. Similar ventilations took place in the trainees' room. When supervisors gathered in their scheduled meeting, they tended to engage in worried discussions which identified specific trainees whose work seemed problematic in some way, with comparatively little reference to the supervisor–trainee dyad or to the network of relationships within the small supervision group as a whole. Such an exploration was not con-sciously withheld, but was not perceived as an ongoing feature of small group life which might be relevant to the work of the supervisors' group.

One possible explanation for this is that an already pressurised supervisor may feel exposed in two ways: as a facilitator for trainees to develop their own styles, and as a representative of the institution in modelling its aims and philosophies. The necessity to hold the tension between these two roles can be exceptionally stressful.

IDENTIFICATION AND IDENTITY

In an institution such as this one, trainees who are judged to be working most successfully are often those whose methods and ideologies do not grossly challenge either the supervisors' institutional loyalty or their faith in their own professional orientation. A particular trainee's differing theoretical convictions or technical approaches may place increasing pressure on a supervisor's internal boundaries, especially when these are based on a benign introject of the institution. At an emotional level, a supervisor may be aware only of a frustrated impatience with a particular trainee's clinical technique, and a desire for the trainee to conform to a 'standard' clinical approach, for example to take up a client's negative transference. Such trainees, sensing the supervisor's irritation and withheld criticism, may seek to postpone the report of a client session by describing counter-transference reactions or client history, rather than allow open access to clinical material which would expose them to their supervisor's critical opinions, which they may experience as excluding them from their fellow trainees.

The same dynamic may occur within staff groups. A positive introject shared by a number of staff members can create a powerful but exclusive unconscious bond. Within one staff group, those supervisors who had trained with the institution, regardless of the fact that they also had alternative training experience, were perceived by the group as a whole as carriers for the ethos of the organisation; those supervisors whose experience did not include a placement at the institution were unconsciously perceived as different, 'alien', and outside the umbrella of established institutional codes of belief. A fantasied hierarchy was in operation in which affinity with the institution was the most valued credential amongst all supervisors; affiliations to other training bodies or faith in treatment methods other than psychotherapy were played down or ignored by the total membership in an unconscious effort to 'homogenise' the group as a whole.

The concept of membership implies fulfilling desired selection criteria, as well as reward for acquiring an institutional identity. At a psychological level, rewards may include freedom from separation anxiety, and relief from paranoid fantasies of expulsion and abandonment. If the group's security is felt to be threatened, for example by changes in procedure which require an accommodation of new routines, or by confusion of role definitions, as was the case in the clinic, a group may react with unconscious attempts to maintain uniformity.

At the start of the particular training period in which changes in the collection and storage of information were implemented, one staff group was simultaneously considering new ways of conducting their regular meetings. Supervisors decided to devote meetings to more lengthy presentations of their work with trainee groups, with a possibility of a more refined focus on actual supervision of their supervision. In practice, however, supervisors' presentations did not reveal more dynamics within the trainee groups; after a trial period, the staff group reverted to its original method of reporting on individual trainees. Perhaps the possibility of more revealing presentations alerted the team to differences in supervision styles, based on their different training backgrounds, which would have been difficult to tolerate; even more strikingly perhaps, for supervisors to be in a more conventional supervision setting was synonymous with being in training, and threatened to generate painful identifications with anxious, inexperienced trainees.

SHARED PROJECTIONS

Hinshelwood (1987) states that the divisions between groups in a community, simply by the fact that they exist, attracts the splitting from which assigned roles originate. In terms of institutional dynamics, as one side of the social structure, trainees were unconsciously assigned the role of dependent beginners, bearing the strains of working with ill people, which not only justified their feelings of intense anxiety but also entitled them to support in the form of supervision. Another side of the structure, the supervisors, became experienced providers of that support, qualified for the role by their professional maturity, which in turn entitled them to work without supervision. The fact that the responsibility attached to this latter role could be burdensome, and accompanied by feelings of inadequacy and uncertainty, had to be denied, at least in the group arena, because in the system's collective fantasy only trainees could justify anxiety and inadequacy. It is worth stressing here that what I am attempting to describe is a shared culture, in which an unconscious division of the psychological labour is designed, if that is the word, to alleviate the effects of overwhelming anxiety on the system as a whole. Jacques identified this typical two-sided structure as a general condition of institutional life; he proposed that it may cause natural inherent boundaries between sub-groups to ossify into barriers within organisations. Jacques recognised that organisations divide into sub-groups to facilitate division of labour, and that communication between sub-groups tends to be restricted. They may interact, but they do not always necessarily communicate (Jacques 1951).

THE INSTITUTION AS CONTAINER

As Zinkin (1989) observes, Bion's fundamental concept of the container and the contained may be fruitfully applied to groups and group processes within institutions.

Fantasy based on primitive defences can increase the gap within groups and between sub-groups. Differences between groups and within groups in terms of working methods and underlying philosophies, which could under other circumstances be explored in order to lessen tension and increase understanding among members, can come to feel intolerable and to threaten existing 'standards' of work. Communication may be seriously distorted by the resulting personal barriers between staff members and between staff and trainees. In such stringent circumstances, personal doubt and lack of confidence may be dealt with by all individuals in the network becoming sealed in their own support system, apparently responsible only to themselves. The image of an eggbox, with an individual cradle for each egg, seems apt here, especially as it implies fragility and the need for protection. Although the box may maintain its integrity as a holding environment, it also serves to keep objects apart. The eggbox symbolises one function of the psychotherapy clinic, a safe container, which the environment may consider a more appropriate one for the client than for the workers. In this case, the client sub-group may safely carry the projected feelings of fragility for staff, trainees, and administration.

In the clinic, at an administrative level, protection for individuals who were considered fragile – its clients – was a particularly high priority at this moment. Consciously, all institutional members recognised that the plan to make files accessible to clients was desirable and democratic. At a scarcely conscious level, the new computer storage system represented a loss of vital privacy for both supervisors and trainees. Up until this time 'control' of session notes had been considered their preserve, despite the fact that they knew that in reality all notes were by rights the property of the institution. At a fantasy level, the new storage system, while designed to protect clients, could also threaten to expose the work of both supervisors and trainees, which is by nature as confidential as the work between client and therapist. At a practical level, staff recognised that the probability of a client actually requesting to see a file was minimal; but if one did so, it would indicate a breakdown of the therapist–client relationship, which would then be a matter of public concern. The institution's permission for greater access for clients was perceived at an emotional level less as an added service to clients and more as an invasion of the supervisor–trainee relationship which threatened to shift projections of inadequacy back into the staff and trainee groups.

As if to reflect this fear of invasion, the supervisor staff group at this time was not able to bring its own particular worries about exposure of work to clients into the open to be addressed and worked through, linked as it was to the deeper anxiety about exposure of personal supervision styles and different training ideologies to the – imagined – critical attitude of colleagues. Thus there was a tension in the supervisor group between the need to share information about each other's backgrounds and experience and the need to protect individuals from the threat of exposure which this increased 'access' would bring. This produced a moratorium on open sharing which meant that staff group meetings were predictable and polite, but with a resulting loss of energy. In this group the energy drain was due to the projection (by definition a depletion of the ego) of inexperience and ineffectiveness into a different part of the system – that of the trainees.

Now of course some trainees will weather this kind of situation better than others. Some are better defended against infectious projections from the system; those that do introject them may be able to find containment and relief within their personal therapy groups. A small but uncounted number can succumb. Perhaps they are actually more fragile, or less defended against the internal pressure inspired by the supervisor as a transference object. (It is not within the scope of this chapter to explore this topic further.)

SELF-ASSESSMENT

In the yearly cycle of the psychotherapy clinic, the assessment process was under way. One feature of this process was that supervisors, and to a certain extent trainees, faced a major role change. The task appeared to be an extension of that which supervisors (and trainees' internal supervisors) performed all year. In practical terms, supervisors as a group had to expand their roles as supportive and reflective educators in order to provide unbiased judgement of the work of trainees (within the group setting), some of whom they did not know at all, and some of whom they had spent a year getting to know in contexts of trust and intimacy. The midwife became a gatekeeper.

Unbiased appraisal can be difficult to achieve at the best of times. If there is no legitimate forum in which supervisors themselves may be appraised constructively, they may unconsciously seek from an assessment process the very affirmation and constructive criticism they offer trainees. One way for supervisors to enhance their self-esteem is to make a direct correlation between their own values and the quality of the trainees' work. This may lead supervisors unconsciously to idealise trainees, offering general overall approval and emphasising strengths but remaining blind to weaknesses. Or a supervisor, intending to be supportive, may unwittingly set up competition between trainee groups with observations such as 'We've not lost a client from this group yet'.

Assessment can feel like a trial for those undergoing it; trainees especially tend to project harsh superego attitudes on to supervisors and the institution itself. But when the process is handled with firmness and tact it can provide essential guidance and reassurance and an opportunity to reintroject positive parental images, arising from the myth of the institution as a family structure (Meltzer 1986). Trainees may openly acknowledge their performance anxiety around assessment, along with their need for their supervisor's praise and reassurance. Supervisors however, particularly in an institutional culture, may have only a tenuous grasp of their community self-worth. As a consequence, some may bury their 'internal trainee' and so lose touch with their own need for vital psychological supplies. The assessment process leaves them stressed and depleted, with vague feelings of failure, uncertainty, and perhaps barely conscious envy of trainees who are being held and nourished. Some supervisors, in an effort to achieve a balance, may invite feedback on their supervisory skills from their trainee groups, but in doing so they risk creating more splits between sub-groups, as they could be seen to be offering an opportunity not available from other supervisors.

So far, this account has taken up institutional concerns about how information is collected and stored (the institution as container), and how individual identification with institutional roles is formed and expressed (membership). In the psychotherapy clinic these two linked themes were now running parallel through all levels of the institution – administration, training staff and trainees.

The next section recounts a supervision session with four trainees which reflects these themes, illustrating the way in which one organisational sub-group may mirror other groups' concerns and anxieties. This dynamic may go unremarked by the collective membership of the institution, but will nevertheless affect ways in which sub-groups interact and communicate, or not.

SUPERVISION SESSION

The supervisor had suggested a review of a new group's work over a period of three months. Although trainees and supervisor had had one-to-one contact previously within the institution, none of the four trainees had worked together before.

> Frankie began the discussion by confessing that she had been very anxious when the group had started three months previously because she had been aware of the power of the men in the group (including the supervisor). She had felt that she didn't fit in on several counts – her gender, her occupation as a violinist and her wish to apply for a PhD with a prestigious university in the East. She felt that the supervisor, together with Vince and Nathan, formed a 'little triumvirate', based on their sex solidarity, and when she had to be absent for a few weeks she imagined the group got on better without her. She found her anxiety decreasing as the group settled down; she felt the group respected her work and she was grateful for their praise.
>
> Vince, whose chemistry degree and previous occupation as a highly paid management consultant contributed to the group's perception of his personal power, said that the way Frankie was able to think diffusely and intuitively rather frightened him, and he wished that he could say things the way she did.
>
> Frankie then admitted that she had been worried about how to tolerate Vince's way of working, as she felt she was more intuitive and imaginative, often free associating to her clients' material, while she perceived Vince as more comfortable with theory and more 'dynamic'. The supervisor observed that Vince and Frankie had been noticably irritable with one another in the early days of the supervision group, and how this had felt painful but energetic. He felt there was more potential for expressing differences now that they had brought it into the open. Anna, who came from a nursing background, now turned to Vince, 'At first I thought there was a real man–woman thing going on between you two (meaning Frankie and Vince), and I felt really left out. But I've come to

value your way of working. I find it tremendously helpful, even though it's so different from my own.' She went on to explain her own concern in the group: she felt very dependent on session notes to present in supervision, and she would spend a long time trying to record everything that went on with a client in considerable detail so that she could 'give the group enough to get into'. She was afraid that if she departed from her notes she would simply present the group with a 'mess' of impressions and feelings.

Nathan, who had remained silent until now, said that he was more concerned about the end of his placement period which was coming soon; he wanted to start a psychotherapy practice in the nearby capital but he wasn't sure whether his qualification from the clinic was sufficient to enable him to support himself in a very competitive field.

'Of course, that is a subject of concern for the clinic as well,' Frankie said.

'I'm standing in for the clinic then!' Nathan replied.

Vince said that, like Nathan, he was also anxious about taking notes, but for a different reason. His father, uncle and grandfather had worked for the federal law enforcement agency in the state capital, and supervision for him felt as if he was in a court of law having to defend himself. The group was both judge and jury. Frankie wanted to know what his crime was.

'I don't know,' Vince said, furrowing his brow, 'I only know that whenever I present in supervision I feel exposed and nervous, as if I'm going to be caught out.'

'Maybe that's why you always want someone else to go first?' Anna suggested, 'I know I look to Frankie to start us off.'

The supervisor suggested that Vince felt in need of an advocate, and that he might be carrying something quite important for the group.

Discussion

Broad concerns of entitlement to membership and the need for adequate containment emerge in this supervision session. In preparation for this session the supervisor had met each trainee individually, asking each to think about communication processes within the group by considering questions such as: Who speaks to whom? Who listens? Which trainee chooses to present first? Are some trainees favoured more than others in terms of time or attention? Group members were encouraged at the individual meetings to report their concerns to the group review. The tension between two trainees due to their different working styles had been evident in the group but could now be acknowledged openly by all members. Anna's ingenuous support and the supervisor's calm validation helped to contain splits, and decrease persecutory fantasies of exclusion and abandonment. Anna's comment, by demonstrating mastery of her envy, enabled Frankie to see, later in the session, that her remark about the triumvirate disguised her own enviousness.

The trainees' need to share information, both personal and professional, was evident in the group review and was partly held in check by one member's need for protection from overexposure.

While all members could relate to the internal pressure of this shared tension, it was Vince who was able to voice it as transference to the supervisor and the institution.

The trainees themselves identified the correlation between their concern about the validity of their professional identities and the wider issue for the clinic in its relation to the community it served. The fact that Nathan perceived that he was reflecting an issue that was shared by the clinic as a whole made him feel less isolated and insignificant.

Anna's worry about her notes reflected her conflict about how to contain very sensitive material while allowing the group sufficient access to it, and of course to her. This was her own personal reflection of the wider issue for the institution which had inspired the administration to instal new computers, and which, at the staff level, had led the staff group to attempt a different presentation approach in their regular meetings.

Vince feared being judged by an authority that was 'gathering evidence' about his performance without sharing it with him, a transference from his family of police officers to his supervisor, as well as the bureaucratic face of the institution. His fear indicated a possible identification with the clinic's clients before they were allowed access to their files; his reluctance to speak and write notes mirrored the block experienced by supervisors in their group.

Within the trainee group, members were assigned different roles, for example, facilitator, spokesman, critic, in order to address their common anxiety, just as within the institution itself sub-groups took up different aspects of the psychological work of coping with the stress of institutional life. The tension between trainees within their group mirrored a similar state in the supervisor staff group. The trainees were able to acknowledge their differences when other trainees' styles were proved effective and the group could see that the supervisor valued them all.

Factors which facilitated this experience were the relatively small size of the group and the fact that all trainees were at the same training level. Other variables, such as how well they knew each other and had contact outside the group, were difficult to determine but could also have influenced cohesiveness within the group itself. It is noteworthy that one trainee group had absorbed, through psychodynamic processes, anxieties relevant to the whole institution and had brought them into group consciousness. In fact, although we have been focusing on two of the many sub-groups within the clinic, every sub-group was attempting, with a greater or lesser degree of consciousness, to face institutional anxieties and master them. As the example of the supervision session demonstrates, each individual represented a nexus or focal point for the anxieties and concerns shared by the whole institution, a microcosm reflecting the macrocosm. As each individual heightened his or her consciousness, the potential for collective awareness within the institution was enhanced.

The model used by the trainee group, in which individuals spoke first of their reactions to the group in one-to-one meetings arranged by the supervisor, and then reported their conversations back to the whole group, is an effective technique in group analysis. This approach acknowledges that vital, energetic exchanges between group members are an inevitable occurrence outside the group container but, in this case, still within the wider context of the institution. Members are encouraged to return the energy to the group. An ongoing ebb and flow of energy and information is therefore established as a model for each sub-group; institutional life flows within groups and between groups, which reflects the dynamic of projection and introjection within the internal world of each individual.

CONCLUSION

In terms of institutional dynamics, one part of the system, in this instance a supervision group, was able to mobilise positive impulses in the form of candour and tolerance, in order to counteract the defensive system in the group. One essential task for this group was to face the reality of the climate they were inhabiting through an open exploration of the feelings of members. Taking responsibility for each other in this way improved morale and increased feelings of effectiveness. Positive concern and a non-punitive attitude, as modelled by Frankie and Anna and supported by the supervisor, helped the group to overcome their guilt at the hostility towards each other due to differences in clinical approaches. They could then begin to further explore shared anxieties and to promote a genuine exchange.

REFERENCES

Bion, W.R. (1961) *Experiences in Groups*, London: Tavistock Publications.
Hinshelwood, R. (1987) *What Happens in Groups*, London: Free Association Books.
Jacques, E. (1951) *The Changing Culture of a Factory*, London: Routledge & Kegan Paul.
Meltzer, D. (1986) 'The analytical world: institutions and limitations', *Journal of Analytical Psychology* 31(3): 264.
Zinkin, L. (1989) 'The group as container and contained', *Group Analysis* 27(3): 227–234.

Chapter 13

Supervision in the organisational context

Marlene Spero

This chapter is based on some of my reflections as a supervisor to students, managers and staff working in different organisations who were interested in looking at their work from a psychodynamic and group-analytic point of view. The objective of the seminar was to extend the participants' awareness of individual and group dynamics to an understanding of organisational dynamics, and to focus on tasks, roles, relationships, communication patterns and wider systemic issues, namely the organisational matrix. The case material illustrates some of these issues and some of the problems that staff have to contend with in their everyday working life. Comments are also made about the supervision group as a tool of learning and development.

THE CONTEXT

The members of the seminar came from a variety of backgrounds including hospitals and psychiatric units, business organisations, the clergy, social services and voluntary agencies. Some had a knowledge of psychoanalytic and group dynamic theory but others did not. In their work lives they were faced with issues of organisational change, mergers, conflicts with bosses or colleagues, feelings of insecurity and ambivalence, confusion and chaos.

The sessions were always very rich. The case material provided a wonderful opportunity to reflect on and think about very different organisations and their problems in a non-threatening way. Working with a group of colleagues made it easier to talk more openly and to share anxieties and uncertainties than would have been the case in a supervisor–supervisee situation where issues of dependency and authority prevail. The members were able to exchange knowledge and skills so that the whole experience became a very creative one, both deepening and widening the level of understanding and insight.

As a supervisor, I felt that in many ways I was another colleague with a different body of knowledge, experience and skills helping the members to reflect on their work. I was less of a transference figure and more of a leader containing the group and holding the boundaries. The distance between myself and the members was lessened as the group was not dependent on me and I was not seen as the expert. I was a role model and would ask questions, make interpretations and encourage the group to look at what was happening in their work and in themselves from different conceptual points of view. I would also take a more active role and make concrete suggestions if necessary.

My task was:

1 To facilitate the free flow of discussion, communication and thinking.
2 To create a safe space for the members to experiment and take risks.
3 To develop their understanding of themselves, both in and out of role, as well as of their organisations, and to enable them to function more effectively in role.
4 To make links between some of the theoretical ideas and concepts and the practical work that was presented.

The seminar was based on psychoanalysis, group analysis, systems theory and sociology. Thus concepts like splitting, denial, projection, regression were used to enable members to look at their work. The group process was explored as well as the organisational matrix roles, relationships, boundaries, communication and feedback systems, culture and the wider political, social and economic influences. Reference was made to the work of Jacques (1953), Lyth (1988), Bion (1961), Foulkes (1984) and the Tavistock Institute (Trist and Murray 1990).

There were four to seven members in each group. The groups met weekly for one and a half hours; time was structured, however, in that one member would present for an hour and the rest of the time would be used for any other concerns that members may have had. Associations began to flow and links were made as the material presented resonated with their own experiences. The groups worked at different levels of understanding and communication depending on the degree of 'psychodynamic' sophistication available to enable latent processes to be brought to the fore. The content would tend to shift from organisational and wider contextual issues, to problems of role and then the self. In Foulkesian terms, instead of looking at intrapsychic processes, the focus was on intragroup and intergroup and extragroup processes – looking out as opposed to looking in, as would be the case in a clinical seminar. The seminars would on occasions be used to develop training programmes or policies and procedures. The group was also used as a mirror to reflect on behaviour and feelings that on occasions could block thinking within the session. Members were encouraged to explore their counter-transference feelings as well as transference issues and in particular their difficulties in handling authority.

THE CASE MATERIAL

The case material, extracts from the first two sessions of a new group, highlights some of the issues that a seminar group had to tackle, which are typical of the problems faced by organisations and their staff. It also illustrates the group process.

The group consisted of two psychiatric nurses working in day hospitals (T and S), a midwife responsible for a hospital bereavement counselling service (J), a counsellor working in a psychotherapy institute (P) and a counsellor (R) working in a home for single mothers and babies.

> T began by describing his day hospital which serviced the whole of area 'X' and 'all sorts of psychiatric disorders'. The day-to-day activities were run by staff nurses and occupational therapists under a joint management team and four or five different consultants. This was the source of enormous conflict; there were hierarchical difficulties and boundaries were not clear: 'Higher level people just don't talk to each other. There is a constant fight over everything.' I pointed out how these conflicts were often played out further down the organisation. As a result of the recent NHS reorganisation, the hospital was now an independent trust totally responsible for its own functioning. T was responsible for a health discussion group which he ran with an occupational therapist. It was run on non-structured lines and was considered to be quite an innovative thing to do in a culture where everything was highly controlled and structured. The previous group had failed for this very reason, not having met the needs of the participants. S wanted to know what the task of the group was. T said that 'it was to look at health issues including drugs, alcohol, food, the Mental Health Act and medical treatment in general. The patients can discuss anything although personal things have to be dealt with elsewhere.' S said, 'Well, that's a contradiction. It will be difficult for

you to keep the boundaries if you are not clear where they should be.' T continued saying that the management wanted the day hospital facilities open to everyone and consequently several very disturbed inpatients had joined his group. He was anxious about the safety of the group. R said, 'The boundaries are confused.' T agreed, saying that he was in favour of having inpatients but he was never given any case notes. 'There was no way of getting any information – the nurses didn't have time. I would like to set up a forum to do this. They don't have groups upstairs. I want to include them to give them a better life.'

The group began to explore the difficulties of having a joint management structure, and the reorganisation. The culture had changed and there was a clash between professional and business values. Every activity had to be financially viable and this caused enormous resentment. Boundaries were no longer clear and T said he didn't know to whom he could go for support. He felt pressurised by management into doing something that had not been thought through and, as he said, 'had been introduced for the wrong reasons'. I said to T that perhaps his own altruistic wishes were confusing the issue too. He said he hadn't thought of that. I added that it seemed to me that so many of us in the helping professions seem to feel that we need to save everyone but the reality is that we can't. This was acknowledged by the rest of the group.

P then spoke about her organisation. She had been appointed because of her psychodynamic training but once 'in role' had to face the anger and resentment of the course manager. Boundaries between staff and trainees were unclear and P had reorganised them. She also decided to run her training group on analytical lines without a structure. This was something new. The students were furious and reported her to the course manager, who then told P off at the weekly staff supervision session in front of all her peers. She felt attacked, undermined and scapegoated, and was anxious about the next session with the group. T said, 'Well, she is very envious of you – you have a specific expertise which they don't have which makes you very powerful.'

I felt that after the first session the scene was beginning to be set in the way that we would be exploring the group members' roles, organisations and feelings. Common themes were beginning to emerge and the group began to ask questions clarifying particular points and making their own interpretations of what was going on.

J presented the following week. She had recently been appointed to head the prenatal and screening unit, one of only three in hospitals in the UK, only to find when she joined the hospital that the unit had moved into another area and that she was now to be responsible for a bereavement counselling service for parents who had lost babies. She was very angry as she felt she had been misled and as T said 'cheated'. She felt quite ambivalent about the idea of having to take on bereavement counselling even though she had been trained as a bereavement counsellor. The hospital chaplain and a sister had been responsible for the counselling to date and she described them as feeling very threatened by her. She was better trained and as soon as she attempted to introduce any new procedures they would sabotage them. She would leave details and explicit instructions for their distribution but the information was never passed on. J was furious. She also discovered that the chaplain would do as she pleased and did not actually have a job description.

J decided that the best way to implement the changes would be to set up a multi-disciplinary group and involve as many of the staff as possible who were interested. She invited all those from the relevant teams. There had been changes in the abortion law and it was important that a new policy should be put into place. She said, 'What could have taken me two weeks is going to take two years.' The group resonated with this saying that they too had experienced enormous difficulties in getting any new ideas accepted and as a result had felt incredibly frustrated and de-motivated. J didn't really want the group but thought it would be politically the best thing to do. She invited the chaplain and sister to participate but found that they tended to dominate the meetings, resisting many of the suggestions that she would put forward. She felt deskilled and wanted to resign as chair but was concerned that things would revert back to how they were before. She was also very angry that whatever she did had to be vetted by two other committees and felt that her hands were tied in every direction.

T immediately said that he understood how difficult it was for her to be accepted by the unit and recalled that when his hospital was made a trust, 'new people' came in from outside with new ideas which made it impossible for him. He felt quite paranoid. T then said that 'Staff often feel just as crazy as their patients; they get all the feelings dumped on them.' R said she experienced the same distress and confusion with the residents in her home and that it was very important that this should be taken back to those involved and worked with. The group went on to explore their own resistance to change. P said, 'Well, the whole thing is about power. You have all the power because you have the expert knowledge. That is what they resent. It's a fight for power; they think you are taking it away from them.' She was totally identified with J. This is exactly what she was experiencing herself. S said, 'Your department is like the "jewel in the crown"; they say that about mine and it causes lots of ill-feeling. People get envious.' R, referring to the group, said, 'How is it ever going to work if you don't really want to be doing it?' The members then went on to explore their own ambivalence about their work and the difficulties of working with bosses and systems that were insensitive to the needs of clients as well as staff. I added that one of the things that seemed to add to the confusion and stress was the lack of boundaries. The group also helped J to explore why she felt so deskilled and ineffective in the group. She realised that she was introjecting all the in-competent feelings of the chaplain and the sister.

S then described his day hospital which he felt was far better organised than T's. It was referred to as the 'jewel in the crown' but the reality was that it was just as chaotic as T's unit. The unit had just moved to a new location; it had a long-established five-day programme with lots of different groups as well as a support system. The unit had always been psychodynamically orientated and concerned with understanding how organisational dynamics and processes impinged on the work. Management, he said, got on well. After presenting a rather idealised picture of his unit, S then went on to describe how he had had to run groups without any training. He worked with a charge nurse and although time was allocated for debriefing after the group there was never enough time as three groups had to be discussed. He also had six patients in individual therapy and again did not feel that he was getting proper supervision and said he felt very stirred up. T was amazed and said, 'What do you do with your feelings? How can you cope?' S said, 'But we do have the structures.'

I spoke about structures in institutions being defences against anxiety and reminded them of Lyth's (1988) paper.

T went on to say, 'But you need an outside observer to see what is going on inside. If you are in the middle of it all, you can't see. How can your unit be so special if you don't have sufficient support?' I was aware that the two men were quite rivalrous.

Finally R talked about her mothers and babies home and the splits between the new and old staff and the differences in attitudes. The older staff would encourage dependency and 'mollycoddle' the residents, whereas the new staff wanted to make the residents independent so that they could go back and live in the community. As one of the group pointed out, 'Perhaps the older staff don't want to lose numbers as the place would surely be closed down if they did.' R hadn't thought of that. There were only six mothers in residence and the home catered for twelve. There were funding difficulties and she felt very vulnerable. She also said that she felt she was resented because she was middle class and had a degree. She wasn't sure whether she would have a job next week. The group suggested that she presented the following week so that they could explore more deeply what was going on for her. I wondered if they were trying to rescue her like their patients.

At the end of the second session I was aware that boundaries were an issue for the group. Would they feel safe? I hadn't as yet consciously decided to use their work as case material but maybe this was already in the matrix at a sub-conscious level. The group was beginning to pair and to become quite rivalrous. There was also a high level of anxiety and frustration and I was aware of the need for the supervision seminar to act as a container. Common themes were beginning to emerge and con-nections to be made with their organisations, with their roles and with themselves. The members began to ask very different questions about themselves and their organisations.

CONCLUSION

The sessions began to reveal some of the key conflicts and dysfunctional processes that are part of organisational life and undermine individual motivation and productivity. It is these issues that are looked at in more depth as the seminar progresses so that considerable insight and under-standing is achieved. The group was beginning to explore wider con-textual issues: the impact of changes in government policy on the health care system; cultural change; the conflict between professional and business ethics; the resistance to change; concerns about boundaries; informal networks and issues of power, idealisation, splitting and denial. At a functional role level there were issues of envy, collusion, rivalry, scapegoating and sabotage, and at a more personal level questions of ambivalence, motivation and confidence. These are typical of the prob-lems that staff face working in any organisation.

In presenting the above I have tried to illustrate what goes on in a group-analytic supervision group for people working in the organisations. The focus is on the organisation and its wider context and the presentations move from descriptions of the organisations *per se* and the political, social and economic influences on them, to an analysis of what actually happens in the organisations, looking at the members' roles and finally their feelings about themselves 'in role' at both manifest and latent levels. The individual is always seen in the context of his role and organisation – figure and ground. The process within the supervision group is also used to reflect behaviours in the here and now with the hope that members will experience an enhancement of their egos and become more active and confident in their work roles.

REFERENCES

Bion, W.R. (1961) *Experiences in Groups*, London: Tavistock.
Foulkes, S.H. (1984) *Therapeutic Group Analysis*, London: Karnac Books.
Jacques, E. (1953) 'On the dynamics of social structure', *Human Relations* 6: 3–24.
Lyth, I.M. (1988) *Containing Anxiety in Institutions, Selected Essays*, London: Free Association Books.
Trist, E. and Murray, H. (1990) *The Social Engagement of Social Sciences: A Tavistock Anthology*, London: Free Association Books.

Chapter 14

Training of supervisors

Meg Sharpe

> I can't teach you to do psychotherapy. . . only you can do that. I can only
> teach you how to think about psychotherapy.
>
> (Bettleheim and Rosenfeld 1993: 11)

The selection and training of supervisors is a complex business. Not
every practitioner is cut out for it, nor indeed wishes to be a supervisor.
How can one be sure that those who might supervise others are up to the
job, that those chosen will acquire what is needed to be effective and that
their trainers are equipped to provide it?

It is very important to be able to identify those best suited and motivated
for this task. Students need to be brought to maturity, and in the early days
of training the supervisor is a key person in the educational and developmental experience. During this process the foundation is laid for continuous
improvement in the art of group analysis and the establishment of habits
focused on the practice of enquiring self-scrutiny.

It is evident that the quality of the training processes involved will be
coloured by the calibre of the trainer, and while in what follows I will
deal with some of the basic issues which arise, I shall not address the
question of who trains the trainer.

Although a training programme is being considered, there is as yet no
formal system for training supervisors at the London Institute of Group
Analysis. In the early years new supervisors were approved by the Training
Committee, based on background and experience, and just got on with it
without any substantive input from founder teachers. This both enabled and
required many of us to work out for ourselves how (and how not!) to
supervise; it no doubt produced some casualties on the way.

Approached sensitively, training potential supervisors in small
groups is a rich process. Just as group analysts are individual in their
style, so it is with supervisors. Trainee supervisors (TSs) from different
professional backgrounds will usually enhance the group's potential by

supplying a corresponding variety of perspectives for its work. The main process for the TS is relearning how to function as a member of a team and how to participate fully in an interdependent co-ordinated peer environment. I find the optimum number for such a group is between four and six.

Supervisor training is necessarily by, in and of the group, including its trainer – exactly as in a group-analytic group – and further learning is fostered through a mutually creative group process.

THE TRAINER'S TASKS

Objectives

A primary objective for the trainer in developing the potential of all members of the TS team is to achieve *effective communication* in the widest sense. As an example, the importance of sensory sensitivity in all its forms needs to be recapitulated: stimulation of the ear, acute listening; of the eye, sharpness of observation; of the voice, its timbre and tenor; even of the nose, quality of smell. As illustrations:

- One TS found it somewhat distracting to sit next to a colleague whose feet smelled;
- Another mentioned the intrusive effect of an extensively advertised perfume worn by a female TS – appropriately named 'Poison'!

Such disclosures may not have been possible if the TSs had not been in a group as peers and thus open to comments on important physical affects which their patients would more likely suffer in silence. Galimany (1993) relates a moving example of the effect of the analyst's intonation on a patient, setting in motion significant memories.

Another key objective of the trainer is to encourage discussion and to deepen awareness of the objectives and obligations of supervision, and to keep them constantly in mind.

It is often not easy for established mature group analysts to return to the status of trainees and to have their assumptions on these topics examined and debated. TSs have to confront their own ignorance, being sometimes told what to do, being expected to do it, and to tolerate the anxiety of carrying the responsibility for future supervisors. Their own work is once more under the microscope. Disappointment and disillusion have to be coped with along the way. And while the way can be exciting and interesting, it is also demanding and stressful.

Responsibilities

The trainer assumes responsibility for the following in setting up and developing a TS group:

1 *Structure* – clarity of the contract and the process; the structure will be both implicit and explicit.
2 *Starting* – the trainer may need to take the lead and provide sufficient process material to get things moving in a group that may lack shape at this early stage and whose members may not know each other.
3 *Mid-course* – the trainer now concentrates on maintaining the pace and level of energy. Transference, counter-transference, resistances, anxieties and conflicts will be echoed in the group from the TSs' own material.
4 *Closure* – certain rituals need to be attended to and must not be overlooked, just as an analytic group is prepared for closure.

Talent spotting

How are supervisors to be selected? What qualities are appropriate?

From my own process of 'learning-by-doing' I consider the following criteria useful in selection; they should be checked over before deciding to endorse a therapist's application:

- A number of years' experience in conducting various types of groups;
- A range of experience, i.e. not just stranger groups or NHS groups or social services or counselling groups;
- Evidence of motivation towards raising and maintaining professional standards, and developing students' potential;
- Supporting/working for the Institute on various courses and committees, experimental workshops, block training, postgraduate development;
- A sound knowledge of theory;
- Enthusiasm for passing on and sharing knowledge and experience;
- Clear views on supervision and a preferred approach;
- Written work and publications demonstrating a confident personal stance;
- Respect of peers;
- Teaching talent, the capacity to be a good teacher in action. Good group conductors should in principle make good supervisors;
- A good memory; supervisors need to carry a lot of groups in their heads;

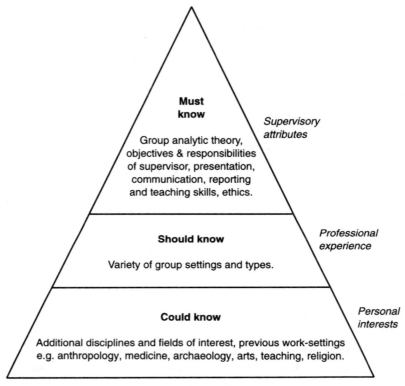

Figure 14.1 Supervisor's knowledge profile

- A coherent personal code of behaviour which will convey to students qualities of integrity, self-awareness, reliability, initiative, empathy, warmth and openness. These attributes make a good analyst; they should also make a good supervisor.

Potential supervisors can become evident at a very early stage, in the cradle as it were. In the final term of Qualifying Course supervision, I sometimes invite students, both here and on courses abroad, to take turns to be the supervisor. This is especially helpful to those students who are launched into supervision at their workplaces immediately on graduation. This has produced some surprising results. For example, a therapist who was competent but not particularly gifted proved to have a special talent as a supervisor – and became authoritative, expansive, holding and creative.

Figure 14.1 attempts to position the trainer's endeavours in relation to the supervisor's overall knowledge and experience profile.

The trainer is of course primarily concerned with filling out the 'must know' apex of Figure 14.1.

Getting the most from the group

To help TSs to develop a wider base for their supervision skills, the full variety of experience in different types of environment which is always present in the group should be drawn out by the trainer (or illustrated from the trainer's experience) for the members to study, share and explore in discussion. Such material may range through hospital, social services, pastoral and industrial or commercial settings, and forms part of the 'should know' area of Figure 14.1.

The profile of the individual TS is underpinned by and differentiated from those of trainee peers by personal knowledge and experience in other fields – e.g. religion, archaeology, anthropology, medicine, art, music, drama, etc. – the 'could know' area, which brings individual quality to the supervisor's style.

'Must know' topics to be studied

There are five main areas of responsibility which the TS needs to be constantly aware of and to have had considerable experience with:

1 Students' patients;
2 Students themselves;
3 The external contexts in which the trainees work;
4 The professional institute;
5 Ethics.

The trainer ensures that each of these is worked on in depth by the TS group.

Responsibility to the patient

To ensure that the highest quality of work is done for the patients of the students they are supervising, the trainer needs to acquire a clear psychological understanding of the members of their groups, as well as supporting knowledge of their backgrounds and reasons for their membership. The trainer is here dependent upon the profiles the TSs produce; they may need help at the initial interview stage in order to make appropriate selections and to take care of the formalities.

Responsibility to the students

Trainers have a responsibility to maintain students' morale and give all necessary help. This means making sure adequate skills in certain management tasks are taught. The TS needs to

- define and hold boundaries;
- set up the mechanics of sessions carefully;
- set a high standard by example;
- know the students well;
- accept responsibilities; and
- be careful about the use of power.

Salvendy (1993) focuses on the relationship between supervisor and supervisee and the inherent use and abuse of power and control in this relationship.

Supervisors who are too 'laid back' may not accomplish much; the positive, enthusiastic supervisor tends to produce good work while the dogmatic, negative, confronting supervisor can produce casualties (although tough students may be stimulated by such a challenge).

Responsibility to the external context

Potential supervisors must be well-versed in how to deal with complex organisations. Every group transacts within a larger setting – a hospital, social service organisation, clinic or practice, factory or office. This environment may be supportive, antagonistic, or indifferent. Some therapeutic professionals tend to be inward-looking and too ready to assume that the outer setting is supportive. It is necessary for supervisors to emphasise to students, first, not to make such assumptions, and, second, to develop and maintain a live awareness of and interaction with the surrounding environment and its requirements and priorities. These are likely to include the right to be kept informed, to be consulted, and to have certain rules and procedures observed.

In a hospital setting, members of the students' group are the clinical responsibility of consultants, doctors and nurses, and the administrative and welfare responsibility of the hospital management. To ignore these external relationships is to court trouble, and to establish a healthy supportive setting for the group and its members, conductors should be prepared to develop the necessary diplomatic and negotiating skills. As an example:

A student expressed anger with the consultant at the hospital where she conducted her group. 'He never sends me any good patients. They are unsuitable and he sees them when he wants to and supports those who complain about me . . .' While sympathetic towards the frustrated student, the group also pointed out that she was a guest at the hospital; had she made any attempt to talk to the consultant about the group, its transactions and what she hoped to achieve? The consultant himself was not a psychotherapist so perhaps she should think about keeping him fully informed, that is, do some PR spadework.

Negotiating and diplomatic skills are an essential part of any effective administrator's armoury, and group conductors, as the perceived 'responsible persons', are the mediating interfaces for their groups and need to acquire these skills. This point seems the hardest to accept for those most committed to 'caring'; it is an issue that cannot be ignored in training programmes. Counter-transference issues are not limited to the therapist; the treatment team is also involved and problems can arise in conflicts with the setting.

Trainee supervisors thus have to be helped to develop skills which can be passed on to their students in order to protect their endeavours when the organisational 'climate' is hostile. The background experience of the supervisor will of course determine the range of advice that can be put forward about survival in autocratic, democratic, bureaucratic and other types of culture.

Negotiation of tolerable space and conditions in order to ensure satisfactory group work has to be brought home to the sometimes naive or too compliant student and also, indeed, to the supervisor-in-training.

Example 1 – One trainee related his despondency and lack of enthusiasm for his task. Among other variables that evolved in discussion was the fact that he supervised at a large hospital in a room that resembled a 'slit trench', no windows, dirty paint on the walls, bad lighting, uncomfortable chairs. He felt disabled and claustrophobic, resentful of the seeming disrespect shown by the institution towards group psychotherapy. The TS group suggested that he look at his inner world; perhaps there would be an explanation for his acceptance of such bad conditions. Did he not value himself sufficiently to negotiate better space? He would not conduct an analytic group there, so why had he not looked after his supervision group better?

Example 2 – A TS reported a difficulty often encountered in a psychiatric setting. One of her students, X, reported that most weeks a disturbed long-stay patient, N, deeply resentful of the time the therapist spent with 'outsiders', would warn off group members as they arrived for the outpatient group. N waited in the lobby, pretending to be 'crazy', and screamed out to individuals as they arrived, 'Don't go to that group, X is dangerous and mad.' X remained fairly tolerant of N's outbursts until one new group member turned tail and fled from the hospital. Action had now become necessary.

Ideas flowed from the TS group and a good compromise evolved. The TS was advised to talk to X, suggesting a meeting with N, and if necessary offer to give N individual attention *after* the group if she stopped harassing its members. The result was that most of the time this worked; N waited silently (albeit gloweringly) and eagerly accepted her space later; five minutes' attention was enough. Eventually N focused her energies elsewhere.

Encouraging students to stay wide-awake to the political currents that flow within all organisations and which shape events which can affect their groups, and also to develop survival skills, is essential. Examples of organisational obstruction are useful, and illustrations of defeat can be as valuable as those of victory.

Role-play of organisational conflicts can also be very instructive. A setting is chosen, roles assigned (based on difficult real-life characters known to members of the supervision group), and a particular problem-situation affecting a therapy group is set up (again, based on an actual experience if possible). 'No-holds-barred' role-play, subsequently analysed by the trainee supervisors with guidance from the trainer, is a powerful development tool.

In summary, the main topics to cover in this important area include:

- The part the therapy groups are perceived to play within the organisation;
- The 'climate' around the group – positive and negative aspects. Who, if anyone, is the conductor answerable to?
- Who control(s) the immediate setting of the group and availability of its members?
- Identifying allies and opponents. Who feels threatened by the group's existence?
- Mustering support/fostering alliances: 'playing politics';
- Planning actions to solve problems and minimise trouble;
- Negotiating through conflicts;
- Maintaining a good climate around the group and keeping the 'outside' in the picture.

Students will bring to their sessions problems and attitudes shaped by working environments which raise issues in all the above areas. In their training group, supervisors may find there is much to be learned from the experiences of others that can be used elsewhere.

Responsibility to the training institute

This body pays the bill for the supervision of its students. As its agent, the supervisor undertakes to supervise effectively and provide reports, to observe the ethical code of the institution, to accept and support its goals and to enhance its professional standing.

Providing reports and assessments

Most supervisors are required to report students' progress to the Training Committee of the respective institution. These reports are intended to convey a clear picture of the development of the student that will enable progress to be monitored. There are many ways of drafting these. My own preference, which I have practised for many years now, is to encourage students to do their own reports in the group at the required time (Sharpe and Blackwell 1987). If the supervisor is not included in this assessment procedure it will not work effectively or honestly. Inevitably the main difficulty to guard against is creating a mutual admiration climate in which the truth is obscured or difficult to express. Explaining the objective clearly can help; the point of reports is to evaluate performance and to provide a basis for discussing progress and difficulties in order to help the students to progress. In training supervisors, this self-scrutiny can be developed and encouraged in order to prepare them to face personal criticism from their students. The supervisor has a large say in their qualification and needs to be fair and aware of personal bias and counter-transference issues:

> In addition to instruction and demonstration of process, and the deepening of the trainee's own experience of his inner world and its impingement on his relationship with others, the need for the trainee supervisor to be able to deal with all contingencies in the supervision situation does impose a mammoth task on those of us who venture to train supervisors. As Heimann stated, it is the analyst's unconscious that communicates with that of the patient. This can be extended to say that it is the group analyst's job to use his unconscious to identify with that of his patients, and this can be further extended to say that

the supervisor needs to be aware of his counter-transference operating through the trainee to the group.

(James 1979: 45)

By self-assessment in their own training supervision group, trainee supervisors can become more confident in facing criticisms, provided the trainer is open to criticisms too. This openness can be encouraged and developed, but research needs to be done on more effective evaluation methods in order to minimise inherent difficulties. Constant monitoring is necessary so that the supervisor learns how to avoid collusion with the students. The IGA supervisor has to deal with the Training Committee, with relationships between different supervisors and with institutional differences, and to learn to avoid popularity polls. So TSs need help to look at their own difficulties in assisting beginners to become group analysts, to cope with frequent occasions when they will feel helpless or irritated by the students themselves because of their lack of experience; in other words to look at counter-transference and be aware of personal blind spots.

Ethical obligations

An area of great sensitivity and importance to a fully professional supervisor is that of ethics and personal integrity. This difficult topic has such particular significance to supervisors, 'therapists-in-the-making' and, above all, their patients, that it should be dealt with at some length.

Supervisor training is *the* opportune process in which to emphasise ethical standards and to ensure that supervisors are well-equipped to instruct their students. It is important to identify the nature of the ethical problems likely to be prominent in each different modality (individual, group, inpatient, outpatient, hospital, family). The likelihood of legal sanctions is real and increasing, and necessarily broad ethical codes of practice may not always suffice. It is more important to ensure practitioners are made very conscious of the centrality of ethics, both as a pre-training necessity and as part of ongoing training; this includes understanding formal legalities. Supervision is a good early vehicle for this.

Supervisors' ethical standards have a direct bearing on the quality of professional guidance received from them. How can they offer consistent well-informed guidance on ethical questions, not just as occasion demands but as a planned part of training? A supervisor's personal position on ethics needs to be made clear, while encouraging full discussion of the issues that surround them. The effectiveness with which students learn to behave with integrity can be strongly influenced by the personal integrity of the supervisor and the honesty made evident in dealing with problems.

It may be inappropriate to envisage a totally uniform common code that should be transmitted, but the trainer should allow no fudging on important differences of position. These need full discussion as a means of developing both TSs' own and their supervisees' professional integrity, particularly and most especially in relation to the protection of the patients.

With the moves towards registration of psychotherapists in this country, both the UK Council for Psychotherapists and the British Confederation of Psychotherapists have stressed the importance of organisations having appropriate codes of ethics, an appropriate complaints procedure and disciplinary procedures. These umbrella organisations approve individual codes.

The TS group provides an excellent ground for open debate on ethical matters. Such debate can be wide-ranging, as evidenced by the following topics and problems which have frequently surfaced in supervision groups:

1 Legal liability of supervisors and the institution. The need to ensure students have medical cover and malpractice insurance cover.

2 Complaints procedure – a thorough knowledge of complaints procedure needs to be acquired so that transgressions are properly and swiftly dealt with, should they occur. For example, what should be done about unethical behaviour on the part of another professional, who may be a colleague? What access to the Training Committee do students have? Any complaint about supervisors needs to be addressed fully and seriously. Often difficulties with supervisors go back to the student's own personal therapy group and may be resolved in transferential terms there, or the matter may be shelved or ignored.

3 Transferring hospital patients to a private group without consultation with the administration of the hospital concerned. This matter was extensively discussed in one group and it was correctly pointed out that the hospital had overall responsibility for the particular patients, who needed to be discharged from it *before* being transferred to a private group.

4 Is it appropriate and right to let patients know that the therapists are students and being supervised? Patients are often delighted to know that there is a 'third eye' concerned for their welfare.

5   How should students deal with relatives of the patient and intrusive telephone calls? 'To speak or not to speak?' One student was upset at being bombarded by letter and telephone by an angry parent who wanted the person concerned 'to get on with it and behave'. Full discussion with the patient (in the group) about this proved useful.

6   Issues of confidentiality – the use of patients' Christian names only (in supervision) in order to preserve this; procedures to follow in any publication of clinical material.

7   Information to GPs or other bodies – how ethical is it to provide confidential material? Should the patients concerned be consulted first and should they receive a copy of any report that goes out? Patients have the right to see their files.

8   The implications of accepting for treatment friends/relatives of a patient who is already in one of the therapist's groups. This could cause unnecessary difficulties.

9   Seeing a patient after treatment is over – when, if ever? What about possible continuation of the transference?

10 Social contact with patients while they are in treatment – holding boundaries.

11 Examples of unethical behaviour encountered by trainee supervisors include:

(a) a patient in a student's group (under clinical responsibility of the student's hospital and supervisory responsibility of the IGA) is taken into another group by a practitioner without any consultation with the group therapist and with no dialogue about the necessity or harmfulness of this action;

(b) a patient who had been in a group for two years with a student, and who was being held through a very negative transference period, was referred by the GP to another hospital and summarily withdrawn from the group with no notice or consultation whatsoever.

Finally there are the ethical responsibilities supervisors have towards students themselves. Salvendy (1993: 365–366) makes the important point that 'the supervisee–supervisor rapport resembles the patient–doctor relationship, with all the ethical considerations regarding trust and dependency implied'. He discusses the risk of sexual harassment or other sexual improprieties in supervision.

TRAINING APPROACHES – STYLES AND VARIATIONS

In training, a supervisor is invariably influenced by other experiences co-existing with formal training. From my own background I owe much to my years of supervision from the late distinguished psychoanalyst, James Home. He taught us that we needed discipline as well as inspiration. He made us think hard about our task and urged us to acquire the habit of constant alertness.

Similarly, while supervising hospital therapists, my own apprenticeship continued for many years through participation in Dr Clifford Yorke's weekly group supervision seminars which he made both nourishing and immensely stimulating. A method I used then for in-service training was to include a potential supervisor in a supervision group conducted by an experienced supervisor. Following each group, a brief teaching session led by the experienced supervisor would be held, in order to integrate and understand the process and its theoretical underpinnings.

The interesting supervision structure set up in Athens and described by Dr Tsegos in Chapter 11 merits careful study and could well be adapted as a valuable training exercise for trainee supervisors.

Finally I should mention supervision from colleagues, which is a very fertile arrangement. Here, mixing experience and age is beneficial in enhancing stimulation. The old can learn from the young, the jaded from the enthusiastic, and vice-versa. Variety in the texture of the group is a great aid to mutual learning and motivation.

CONCLUSION

While I did not set out to deal with the problems of the trainer as such, it may be appropriate to suggest that trainers also, as part of the essential process of continuing self-scrutiny, take time to reflect on and learn from their own role, their personal and professional identity.

Complacency is the enemy. Issues to bear constantly in mind are those attaching to the dependence of the TSs on the trainer for good reports. Is any such dependency producing defensive manoeuvres which conceal the TSs' reluctance to reveal their own thinking, and hence keep the trainer at a distance? This is often reflected in supervision groups. One TS reported the difficulty he experienced in his own training with one of his supervisors, who continually interrupted his reporting of his group. This induced in him a defensive position – he openly stated it was simpler to give the supervisor what was wanted rather than what actually happened. He was afraid that, as a supervisor, students might do the same to him since he, too, was a controlling personality. This example powerfully illustrates the need for trainers to explore their own behaviour in the TS group and guard against becoming too controlling.

As our understanding of the art of group analysis continues to develop, our training standards will need parallel improvement. Equally, as we formalise policies for ensuring this, so will the demands on the trainer increase. Compared with the USA there is as yet not much in the UK literature in relation to the skills and challenges of teaching group-analytic supervision. The subject needs a broader input and deeper study to help us prepare for the demands of the future.

Like any profession we have to develop, through our training armoury, methods which achieve uniformly high standards of operating competence without discouraging originality and new approaches. Some degree of flexibility is thus desirable, but it is important to remember that our customers – the public at large – will increasingly expect from us clear codes of ethics and uniformly high standards of practice.

Jung (1957: 68) has some words for it: 'No amount of explaining can make a crooked plant grow straight but that it must be trained upon the trellis of the norm by the gardener's art.'

Supervision, the 'third eye', is both a primary means of propagating and cultivating our profession's norms, and an essential safeguard for their continued growth.

REFERENCES

Bettleheim, B. and Rosenfeld, A.A. (1993) *The Art of the Obvious*, London: Thames & Hudson.

Galimany, N. (1993) 'Musical pleasure', *International Journal of Psychoanalysis* 74: 383.

James, D.C. (1979) 'Counter-transference in training', *Group Analysis* 12(1): 45.

Jung, C.G. (1957) *The Practice of Psychotherapy, vol. 16 Collected Works*, London: Routledge & Kegan Paul.

Salvendy, J. (1993) 'Control and power in supervision', *International Journal of Group Psychotherapy* 43(3).

Sharpe, M. and Blackwell, D. (1987) 'Creative supervision through student involvement', *Group Analysis* 20(3): 195–208.

Further reading

Maggie Wood

INTRODUCTORY NOTE

The following references have been selected by the terms 'group psycho-therapy' and 'supervision'. The majority of the references listed refer to the training of individual psychotherapists, with supervision being conducted in peer groups; only a few refer to the training of group analysts. Three books on the individual supervision of psychoanalysts are included for further reading. Annotations have been given for most of the items, but some titles are self-explanatory.

MAIN REFERENCES

Ahlin, G. (1981) 'A model for institutional development towards therapeutic community', *Group Analysis* 14(1): 60–61.
  The pagination refers to section 8 of the article entitled 'Building up systems for training, supervision and internal education'.
Alonso, A. (1993) 'Training for group psychotherapy', Chapter 25 in A. Alonso and H.I. Swiller (eds) *Group Therapy in Clinical Practice*, Washington: American Psychiatric Press.
  Supervision of group psychotherapy is discussed in this chapter, looking at the following issues: 'mitigation of shame', in which the self-esteem of the student is maintained; 'support'; 'opportunity to observe others' experiences'; 'encouragement of competition'; 'expansion of empathic capacity'; 'relief of projective-identification problems'.
Aronson, M.L. (1990) 'A group therapist's perspectives on the use of super-visory groups in the training of psychotherapists', *Psychoanalysis and Psychotherapy* (Special issue: The supervision of the psychoanalytic process) 8(1): 88–94.
  The author looks at the supervision of a group of trainee individual psycho-therapists and comes to the conclusion that 'to participate in a well-functioning supervisory group can be marvellously rewarding to supervisor and members alike'. He feels that the supervisor combined with the group members facilitates more creative insights than the individuals working alone.

Aveline, M. (1992) *From Medicine to Psychotherapy*, London: Whurr Publishers.
Chapter 13, 'Issues in the training of group therapists', looks at the difficulties experienced by novice group therapists when dealing with the individual and collective experiences of a group. Supervision of the training is referred to within the different sections, e.g. 'inexperienced leaders and their problems', 'elements in a balanced training', 'the perspective of the supervisor and his training'. See also Chapter 11, 'The training and supervision of individual therapists', and Chapter 12, 'The use of audio- and video-tape recordings of therapy sessions in the supervision and practice of dynamic psychotherapy'.

Billow, R.M. and Mendelsohn, R. (1987) 'The peer supervision group for psychoanalytic therapists', *Group* 11(1): 35–46.
This discusses the peer supervision group, the continuum from case-centred peer group supervision to group-process peer supervision groups, transference and counter-transference, and the parallel processes in psychotherapy supervision in relation to the experience of the group itself.

Bott, P. (1976) 'Some factors influencing material reported in group therapy supervision', *Group Analysis* 9(1): 45.
A short personal observation by the author, both as supervisee and supervisor, on factors influencing the supervision.

Bott, P. (1979) 'A systems model for group psychotherapy supervision', *Group Analysis* 12(2): 134–136.
Factors influencing the supervision are considered in relation to systems theory as perceived by Kernberg.

Brandes, N.S. and Todd, W.E. (1972) 'Dissolution of a peer supervision group of individual psychotherapists', *International Journal of Group Psychotherapy* 22: 54–59.

Counselman, E.F. and Gumpert, P. (1993) 'Psychotherapy supervision in small leader-led groups', *Group* 17(1): 25–32.
The authors conclude that leadership rather than supervision facilitates the supervision process by maintaining a safe environment for the supervisees.

Dick, B. (1975) 'Facilitating personal change', *Group Analysis* 8(1): 22–23.
This is a report on a small group led by Dr Foulkes at the Third European Symposium on Group Analysis. It is concerned mainly with the problems of co-therapy but also looks at power and problem-solving.

Dies, R. (1980) 'Current practice in the training of group psychotherapists', *International Journal of Group Psychotherapy* 30(2): 169–185.
A review of the literature on the training and supervision of group therapists, with a lengthy bibliography.

Fenster, A. and Colah, J. (1991) 'The making of a group psychotherapist; Needs and goals for graduate and postgraduate training', *Group* (Special Issue: Group methods for enhancing the training of mental health professionals) 15(3): 155–162.
Supervision of group therapy work is dealt with in a small section of this article, which is concerned with the overall training experience.

Glatzer, H. (1971) 'Analytic supervision in group psychotherapy', *International Journal of Group Psychotherapy* 21(4): 437–443.

Grotjahn, M. (1977) 'Observations on training, supervision and consultations', Chapter 15 in M. Grotjahn *The Art and Technique of Analytic Group Therapy*, New York: Jason Aronson.

The title is clear. These are some personal observations presented with candour and humour. It is not a detailed theoretical offering but well worth reading.

Grotjahn, M. (1984) 'Don't treat', *Group Analysis* 17(2): 165.

A witty but pertinent letter to *Group Analysis* from this American therapist.

Gustafson, J.P. (1980) 'Group therapy supervision: critical problems of theory and technique', in L. Wolberg and M. Aronson (eds) *Group and Family Therapy*, New York: Jason Aronson.

Psychoanalysis, outcome research, group and social processes are all considered essential to group therapy. An intensive supervision within the allocated weekly hour is described with the parallel development of the supervisee.

Halperin, D.A. (1981) 'Issues in the supervision of group psychotherapy: Countertransference and the group supervisor's agenda', *Group* 5(3): 24–32.

The counter-transference reactions of the group therapist can inhibit therapeutic work in the group, particularly when beginning a group. The author looks at the facilitating role of the supervisor in helping overcome difficulties.

Kanas, N. (1991) 'Group therapy in Leningrad', *Group* 15(1): 14–22.

Larkin, M., Lieberman, M. and Whitaker, D. (1969) 'Issues in the training of group psychotherapists', *International Journal of Group Psychotherapy* 19: 307–325.

Lewis, K. (1989) 'Teaching gender issues to male/female group therapists', *Journal of Independent Social Work* (Special Issue: Variations on teaching and supervising group therapy) 3(4): 125–139.

McGee, T. (1974) 'The triadic approach to supervision on group psychotherapy', *International Journal of Group Psychotherapy* 24(4): 471–476.

Triadic supervision is the supervision of two co-therapists by one supervisor, which is considered a stabilising factor for both the co-therapists and the patients.

Marohn, R.C. (1969) 'The similarity of therapy and supervisory themes', *International Journal of Group Psychotherapy* 19: 176–184.

Mintz, E. (1978) 'Group supervision: an experiential approach', *International Journal of Group Psychotherapy* 28: 467–479.

Napolitani, F. (1979) 'Co-therapy by alternate conduction and reciprocal supervision', *Group Analysis* 12(1): 52–55.

The Institute of Group Analysis in Rome has co-therapy as part of the training. The difficulties encountered in the transference arising from co-therapy has resulted in the co-therapists conducting the groups on alternate months. It is felt that this frees the conductors to use their individual style, and it is easier for trainees to focus on one conductor. Team meetings are used for supervision of the conductors by both trainees and co-therapists.

Nicholas, M.W. (1989) 'A systemic perspective of group therapy supervision: Use of energy in the supervisor–therapist–group system,' *Journal of Independent Social Work* (Special Issue: Variations on teaching and supervising group therapy) 3(4): 27–39.

Papiasvili, A.A. and Severino, S.K. (1986) 'Senior citizens group: the supervisory process (a case of parallel processes in multiple systems)', *Group* 10(4): 211–216.

Pedder, J. (1986) 'Reflections on the theory and practice of supervision', *Psychoanalytic Psychotherapy* 2(1): 1–12.

Styles of supervision (education or therapy) and of the supervisor are considered. The ideas of Winnicott and Balint are discussed, particularly the work of Balint on group supervision.

Pfeffer, D., Epstein, C. and Herrera, I. (1989) 'Group supervision: A psychodynamic perspective', *Journal of Independent Social Work* (Special Issue: Variations on teaching and supervising group therapy) 3(4): 7–26.

Roback, H.B. (1976) 'Use of patient feedback to improve the quality of group therapy training', *International Journal of Group Psychotherapy* 26(2): 243–247.

A 22-item patient satisfaction questionnaire is used by trainee group therapists for ascertaining their 'effectiveness'.

Salvendy, J. (1985) 'The making of the group therapist – the role of experiential learning', *Group* 9(4): 35–44.

Salvendy, J. (1993) 'Control and power in supervision', *International Journal of Group Psychotherapy* 43(3): 363–376.

The shifting power balance between the supervisor and the supervisees during training is explored, with options for change considered with the skills of both the supervisor and the supervisees being utilised.

Schneider, S. and Berman, M.H. (1991) 'The supervision group of the transitional object', *Group Analysis* 24(1): 65–72.

Two Israeli co-therapists present their group for student interns and show how the emotional development of the interns within the group is related to their professional expertise. By providing the supervision group as a transitional object, the authors contend that anxieties of training, which can seem overwhelming at times, can be contained.

Schuman, E.P. and Fulop, G. (1989) 'Experiential group supervision', *Group Analysis* 22(4): 387–396.

Experiential supervision uses those emotions experienced in the groups conducted by the supervisees and looking at parallel experiences between the supervisor and supervisees. It is considered that this enables more flexibility and openness in the trainees.

Sharpe, M. and Blackwell, D. (1987) 'Creative supervision through student involvement' (with contributions from John Heatley, Michael Hobbs and Jenny Boys), *Group Analysis* 20(3): 195–208.

This is the only article combining the supervisor's and the supervisee's experiences of group supervision in the training experience. By using a flexible model the supervisor was experienced 'as a colleague in a leadership role' which reduced transference but facilitated openness. Questions are raised on:

1 The collective assessment of supervisors.
2 The training of supervisors.
3 The relationship between trainees and the academic staff.

Slavson, S.R. (1969) 'Supervision', Chapter 14 in S.R. Slavson *A Textbook of Analytic Group Psychotherapy*, New York: International Universities Press.

This is a detailed theoretical consideration of the supervision process with no clinical vignettes. It should be read in conjunction with the previous chapter which looks at the personal development of the group therapist.

Tauber, L.E. (1978) 'Choice point analysis – Formulation, strategy, intervention, and result in group process therapy and supervision', *International Journal of Group Psychotherapy* 28(2): 163–184.
The author considers choice point analysis to be a useful research tool as well as being an important structure for the anxious trainee to use in the therapy.

OTHER REFERENCES TO BE CONSIDERED

Caligor, L., Bromberg, P.M. and Meltzer, J.D. (eds) (1984) *Clinical Perspectives on the Supervision of Psychoanalysis and Psychotherapy*, New York: Plenum Press.
Fleming, J. and Benedek, T.F. (1983) *Psychoanalytic Supervision. A Method of Clinical Teaching*, New York: International Universities Press, Inc.
Lane, R.C. (ed.) (1990) *Psychoanalytic Approaches to Supervision*, New York: Brunner/Mazel.

Journals

Clinical Supervisor (1986) 4 (1–2) Special issue: Supervision and Training: Models, Dilemmas and Challenges.
Journal of Independent Social Work (1989) 3 (4) Special issue: Variations on Teaching and Supervising Group Therapy.
Psychoanalysis and Psychotherapy (1990) 8 (1) Special issue: The Supervision of the Psychoanalytic Process.

Index